HELPING CHILDREN FIND THEIR VOICES

A GUIDE FOR PARENTS AND EARLY YEARS PRACTITIONERS

Kate Freeman

Routledge
Taylor & Francis Group

LONDON AND NEW YORK

Cover image: © Jenny Edge

First published 2022
by Routledge
2 Park Square, Milton Park, Abingdon, Oxon OX14 4RN

and by Routledge
605 Third Avenue, New York, NY 10158

Routledge is an imprint of the Taylor & Francis Group, an informa business

British Library Cataloguing-in-Publication Data
A catalogue record for this book is available from the British Library

Library of Congress Cataloging-in-Publication Data
Names: Freeman, Kate (Speech therapist), author.
Title: Helping children find their voices : a guide for parents and early years practitioners / Kate Freeman.
Description: Abingdon, Oxon ; New York, NY : Routledge, 2022. | Series: Words together | Includes index.
Identifiers: LCCN 2021032318 (print) | LCCN 2021032319 (ebook) | ISBN 9781032151731 (paperback) | ISBN 9781003242840 (ebook)
Subjects: LCSH: Children—Language. | Language awareness in children. | Speech therapy for children. | Language arts (Early childhood)
Classification: LCC LB1139.L3 F69 2022 (print) | LCC LB1139.L3 (ebook) | DDC 372.6—dc23
LC record available at https://lccn.loc.gov/2021032318
LC ebook record available at https://lccn.loc.gov/2021032319

ISBN: 978-1-032–15173-1 (pbk)
ISBN: 978-1-003–24284-0 (ebk)

DOI: 10.4324/9781003242840

Typeset in Din
by codeMantra

HELPING CHILDREN FIND THEIR VOICES

Designed to be used either independently or alongside the 'Words Together' storybooks, *Helping Children Find Their Voices* is a guide for parents and practitioners supporting children in the early stages of learning to talk, specifically to understand and use two-word sentences.

Written in a friendly and reassuring tone, the book untangles questions and concerns that many parents and practitioners share around language development, such as whether children are reaching important milestones, whether they benefit from screen-time and dummies, and what to do if there might be a problem.

Key features of this book include:

- Chapters that can either be followed consecutively, offering tips on how to encourage first words and the combining of words into two-word sentences, or dipped in-and-out of according to the individual child's level of development

- Practical information and advice rooted in theory, giving parents and practitioners the confidence and background knowledge to support communication

- Activities that can be integrated into everyday interactions, giving children the opportunity to hear simple sentence structures that they can progress towards in their own speech.

Also available as part of a set, with four colourful storybooks, this guide is an ideal resource for early years practitioners, parents, and those working with children who have delayed speech and language development.

Kate Freeman is a highly experienced speech and language therapist, consultant and former charity director. She is also a mum to three grown-up sons, and a grandmother. Kate's passion is working with children and families, making a difference to their futures.

Kate's career has included working with children, families, groups, local authorities, charities and commercial organisations, providing an insight into the skills of communication and how children learn to talk.

This guide is dedicated to Bryony, Arthur, Chay, Harvey and Sandy, alongside all the children I have cared for and worked with. These people, their families and early years settings have inspired this guide and the focus on words together.

CONTENTS

Contents

INTRODUCTION

Why talking?

The great scientist, Steven Hawking, is quoted as saying:

> For millions of years, human beings lived just like the animals. Then something happened which unleashed the power of our imagination: we learnt to speak and we learnt to listen. Mankind's greatest achievements have come about by talking – its greatest failures by not talking.
> With the technology at our disposal, the possibilities are boundless. All we need to do is keep talking.[1]

Talking is a uniquely human ability. It distinguishes us from other animals. Yet we often don't focus on talking or the skills needed for this to develop.

It is core to our learning, to our friendships, to our life chances and to our long-term happiness, but have you ever thought about how children learn to talk? Have you ever thought about the part that you play in supporting these skills to develop? This is your chance to find out more and to understand how you can help children to find their voices.

The 'Words Together' series

'Words Together' is a set of books for children who are at the early stages of learning to talk. The beautifully illustrated series shows a group of toys in familiar situations. The books can be shared very easily by parents and/or early years practitioners and childminders to help with children's communication and language development.

The series has an accompanying guide. The children's books and the accompanying guide are easily identifiable by the red, circular 'Words Together' badge.

DOI: 10.4324/9781003242840-1

A bit about me

Hello and welcome to this guide for all adults who are looking after young children. You have such an important job to do and you obviously take it seriously because you are wanting to find out the best way to make a positive impact on the child that you care for.

I am a speech and language therapist by training, a parent of three grown-up boys by experience and a new grandmother. I have been passionate about the impact of strong speech, language and communication development since a random choice of sciences and languages at A Level took me to see a speech and language therapist at work in my local GP surgery.

I have worked with children's speech, language and communication for over 30 years, as a speech and language therapist, trainer, writer and consultant. I have worked with a wide range of parents, practitioners, professionals and leaders, thinking about and supporting children's speech, language and communication development. I have also worked with those who struggle with this (children with 'speech, language and communication needs').

Throughout my career and through my parenthood and grandparenthood, I have seen first-hand how good speech and language skills help children develop in life. The research backs it up too: those pre-school children who have large vocabularies and are achieving at expected levels with their communication and language do better at school. They are more able to make friends, understand and express emotions and get to grips with the rules of the home and classroom. They are also better able to learn the technical vocabulary that's used in school for particular subjects, such as maths, science, art, history or geography.

You see, understanding and talking is not just about getting our needs met, expressing what we want or asking questions, it's about so much more than that . . . It's about asking to join in a game, knowing what we are and aren't allowed to do in any social situation, finding out what's for dinner, telling someone what happened when we fall and hurt ourselves, sharing the excitement of a new experience, or concerns that we might have. It's also about developing the voice inside our heads that enables us to plan how to do something, reminds us that we might get in trouble (if we do something that we shouldn't), or helps us think through different choices that we might have to make.

Pretty much everything we do on a daily basis relies on the ability to understand what others are saying and to be able to share our own thoughts, in our own words. We have the opportunity to help our children to gain this incredible skill. We can help to open their world up through communication and to show them the way into other people's worlds, including the world of education.

So, I want to say 'thank you' for joining me on this journey of discovery. Thank you for finding out how best to develop a child's skills so that they have the very best start in life. And thank you from the baby or child who you are looking after now, for giving them the greatest opportunity to develop the power of speech.

Did you know?

Strong speech and language skills are vital to help children get on in life.

They help children to make friends, progress in school, build relationships, organise themselves and ultimately find a job.

About you

The readers of this guide are likely to come from a range of backgrounds, some with lots of knowledge about child development, some with very little.

You may be a parent, grandparent, aunt, uncle, foster carer or early years practitioner/ childminder, or you may be supporting families in their role as carer and educator. You may be a parent with one or more children, or a step-brother, step-sister or step-grandparent. You may be an adoptive parent or be expecting a child in the near future.

Whether you are responsible for one child or many. Whether you have done it all before. Or whether this is your first time. There is always an opportunity to learn something new or to refresh the knowledge that you already have.

There are some parts of this guide that may be more useful to you if you are caring for a child at home and some parts that may be more useful as an early years practitioner/ childminder. I am not anticipating that you will read this guide from cover to cover (although you are welcome to), more that you are likely to dip in and out. You will find some key messages in boxes throughout the guide.

Whatever your situation, you will know that children arrive without an instruction manual. We all learn as we go along. We all have to manage our own emotions and relationships at the same time as getting to know the new little person in our lives.

Remember

There is no such thing as a perfect parent or practitioner, so try not to feel overwhelmed with lots of information.

Just take one or two ideas from this guide to try. Once you have settled with those ideas, try adding another.

As people caring for children at home, it is really important to find support – from friends, members of your family, neighbours, professionals or books and the internet. Some support will be useful and some less useful. Good support will help prepare you for the task of parenting, understanding that this is a difficult task and something that everyone struggles with at different times. This is not said lightly: there are times when each one of us has felt like a failure, even if we look to others like we know what we're doing. As parents, we all try our best; we find out what we can from whoever we can and hope that it's enough.

If I could give myself some advice as a new parent, it would be to take the long view. Much of what we worry about will turn out alright in the end and if it doesn't, there is still time to worry later.

If you are an early years practitioner or childminder taking on the very important role of supporting our children in their youngest years, the work you carry out sets the foundations for children's lives ahead. The importance of the early years foundation stage (or equivalent) is often underestimated, meaning that those who support this key stage are often not valued. This guide recognises the vital work that you do to build attachments, support self-esteem, encourage independence and enable physical and social development and knowledge of the world.

Nobody who is a great scientist, came to that point without learning how water fills up a container and how, if there is too much water, it spills over the side. Nobody who is a great mathematician, learnt algebra without first being able to count how many pieces of fruit are needed for the three-year-olds around a table. Nobody who is a film-star or politician, started their career without first learning how to wave bye-bye, lift their arms up to signal that they wanted to be carried, or learnt how to join words together.

This guide is for you, **all of you**, to help those children in your care and to give you the confidence and background knowledge to support them. It will help you to understand the science of communication development, help you to know what to expect when and to know how best to carry out the invaluable role of supporting children's communication to develop.

A note for you

This guide focuses, in particular, on the important early stages of communication. This is when words are starting to be understood and used, and when words combine together to make short sentences.

We will focus specifically on using words together.

If you only read one section

There is plenty of recent research which demonstrates that how parents, carers and practitioners interact with children and how they support learning makes a significant difference to the children's pre-school years. We can also see how children's development in their early years affects those children's development throughout their whole lives. The better start that we can give children in their very earliest years, the more likely they are to go on to have happy, healthy childhoods and fulfilled lives. This means that starting right now will help you to give the child the best start.

For those of you who are parenting or caring for older children, don't worry: everything that you do now will still have a significant impact – it is never too late to help your child learn to talk. So, there is no better time than now, and no better person than you, to support a child's communication skills.

Top tip

Talking and playing with a baby as soon as they are born will have a direct impact on helping them learn to talk.

You help develop important skills every time that you spend time communicating with a baby, toddler, or young child. Every time you say something, every time you respond to a sound or words that they say, every time you pull a funny face or wink at them, you are helping to build pathways in their brains that will support their communication skills for life.

Figure 0.1

One particular way of supporting communication is through sharing books with children. This guide is part of a series of books, which focus on supporting communication development through books. The 'Words Together' series includes a set of illustrated books for children. The series focuses particularly on the key stage in communication development that involves joining words together to make the child's very first sentences.

The chapters in this guide are arranged to help you to identify key information about why learning to talk is important, what talking involves and how it develops (Chapter One). The guide then highlights what you can do to help a child learn and use their first words and join words together (Chapter Two). The important two-word stage is discussed in Chapter Three, along with games and activities to encourage learning at this level. Chapter Four highlights other things to think about regarding communication development and Chapter Five helps to think through any difficulties that might occur. The final chapters (Chapters Six and Seven) will help you to plan next steps and identify additional places to find out more.

Whether you read this guide from cover to cover or go to the chapters that are most relevant to your situation, you will come across ideas and tips on encouraging children's talking. There are some general ideas that are helpful to remember, whatever the age of your child or stage of their language development:

Handy hints

- **Give children time** – whether it is a newborn baby trying to copy you as you stick out your tongue, or a 7-year-old explaining how he built a castle at school – time is what all children need. This helps them feel listened to, with no pressure to 'hurry' what they have to say. As a parent of three, I know too well time is not always in good supply. So there are times that children may need to know 'I can't listen right now ...' Let them know you will listen later: 'Let's talk about your castle when we get home.' Then ensure you do.

- **Model good communication** – this means demonstrating the type of talking you want to hear: if you are going to encourage a child to be better at listening, they need to see what that looks like when you listen. If you want them to use new and interesting words, you can use new words to talk about people, events, places and objects and to explain what they are. This applies to babies too – show them how to take turns by listening to them when they make noises. Then you copy the child. You will see that they will copy back – children are great mimics.

- **Know what to expect** – have some idea of how and when children's communication skills develop. There is plenty of information available. Use this information to help support the child. You will find lots of tips in this guide.

- **Watch out for too many questions** – as adults we often confuse finding out what children can do with finding out about the child's interests. We may end up bombarding them with questions – 'What's this?', 'What colour is that?', 'What are you drawing?' It's useful to balance questions with other ways to encourage conversation, such as comments or observations.

- **Most importantly** – HAVE FUN! Conversations and communication can help you to get to know the little person in front of you. Enjoy looking at the world through their eyes, make conversation light and enjoyable. Focusing on talking should feel fun and enrich your relationship. It should not feel like hard work!

Your role...

I'm sure I am not alone in wanting all children to succeed as well as they can. For this, we need to give them the best start in life. This book is focused on helping to do just that. The aim of this book is to help all children to develop good communication skills, through letting important adults know what to do. The activities will benefit all children, no matter how easy or difficult they find learning to talk.

So, your role is clear: You can make a massive difference to a child's life and their future. The support with communication skills that you give now will help them in their early years, and it will last them for the rest of their lives. Once you know how, you will help a child to learn to talk and you can both have fun in the process!

I wish you all the very best in your journey.

Important things to know

✓ Talking is something we are hardwired to do – although many children struggle. You can never be too good at communicating with others.

✓ Talking is important for learning, making friends, getting what you need (and want), making relationships, enhancing learning and education ... The list is endless.

✓ Talking is complex. It involves a range of different aspects – speech, language and communication. Each aspect has different features, and all interact so that we can talk and have meaningful conversations with each other.

✓ Parents, carers and early years practitioners have a vital role to play in supporting children's talking.

✓ All children benefit from support and encouragement, just as with any other skill – and the rewards for good communication are wide-ranging.

Note

1 https://www.ted.com/talks/simon_bucknall_why_public_speaking_should_be_taught_in_schools (14mins 40secs in)

Chapter one

WHAT WE NEED TO KNOW ABOUT TALKING

In this chapter you will learn:

- Why we need to think about helping children to talk

- What talking actually involves

- The components of talking – speech, language and communication

- Why talking is important for our children

- How talking builds brain connections

- How children learn to talk, including key milestones.

Do we need to think about helping children to talk?

Often, when we think about helping children to find their voices, we may hear people say that surely talking is something that doesn't need to be 'taught'. Many people have the view that this is something that children will learn to do naturally. It's true that we appear to be 'hardwired' to communicate, but talking is a skill like any other – just like riding a bike or doing up our buttons. All these skills benefit from encouragement, practice and plenty of support.

Learning to talk doesn't just happen on its own. It is the final stage of a complex process involving the interaction of neurons, social, physical and environmental factors… as well as a whole lot of opportunity!

Learning to talk, or more specifically learning the skills of communication, is as vital in the 21st century as it has been for hundreds of years, if not more so. Almost everything we do in our lives relies on our communication skills – reading; writing; relationships; learning;

DOI: 10.4324/9781003242840-2

employment; understanding the world around us; accessing radio, television, computers and phones; buying and selling; organising ourselves; entertaining; and having fun.

Think about what you have already done today – who have you spoken to, or listened to (in person or on the phone, through TV or radio)? And how much planning have you done for what you are going to do next? It would be very difficult to get through even a small part of our day without the skills of communication.

Government reviews (including those by Frank Field[1], Graham Allen[2] and Dame Clare Tickell[3]) highlight the importance of good communication and language development. These skills are seen to help children at home, in school, in preparation for reading and writing and later in life. They are also important in increasing social mobility and improving life chances.

One of the most important gifts we can give our own children, or the children that we look after, is the gift of effective communication skills. These skills are essential to make our way through each and every day and through life. The impact of not having these skills can be devastating and life-long.

> **Research shows ...**
>
> ...children with good speech, language and communication skills have much stronger chances of making friends.
>
> They are also more likely to be confident, with greater self-esteem.
>
> These children are more able to learn in school and, ultimately, more likely to succeed academically and to live independent lives.

So, you can see how important these skills are for children. And you, as important adults in the child's life, have a key role to play in helping support their development. (Visit Chapter Two to find out particular ways that you can do this.)

What does talking involve?

Talking seems like a simple thing – one that we all take for granted. But speaking and communicating with the people around us is one of the most complex skills children will ever learn.

There are lots of words that describe talking – speech; language; communication; talking; chatting; saying; listening; understanding; conversing. They all sound like they mean the same thing, but there are some specific differences. It is helpful to be clear about what the different aspects of talking are. This way we can understand what's involved and how all the elements interlink.

Having a conversation relies on three main elements – speech, language and communication. All of these elements contain different building blocks, enabling us to build up the skills to communicate with each other effectively.

What is language?

Technically, when we talk about 'language', we mean the words and sentences we understand and speak. You might think of language as being like the languages you learned at school – French and German etc. You might also think about people who speak different languages, their 'mother tongue' as well as English.

In terms of children's development, we use the term 'language' to refer to both understanding what other people say (sometimes known as comprehension, or receptive language) and speaking (often known as expressive language). This can be in English, Urdu, German, Arabic or whatever is spoken around us.

Talking is made up of lots of different pieces, that we (usually subconsciously) fit together, like a puzzle.

Figure 1.1

By '**understanding**' we mean;

- processing words and making sense of what people say;

so when an adult says, 'Go and get your ball from the drawer in the shed' – we know the object being spoken about – ball; the place they can be found, the drawer; and where that is – in the shed. Because of the verbs they use, 'Go and get', we know they want something to happen. All of this information needs to be processed and understood for the action to take place.

- understanding the grammar used:
  - that the order of words being spoken can change meaning, e.g. 'The horse bit the girl' or 'The girl bit the horse';
  - that words can be used to represent phrases, e.g. 'The teddy bear was broken, **its** leg had fallen off';
  - that adding an additional sound changes the meaning, e.g. cat(s).

By '**speaking**' we mean;

- using individual words
  - to say what objects are, e.g. dog
  - to describe the objects, e.g. fluffy
  - to describe actions, e.g. barking
  - or the nature of those actions, e.g. loudly
- using these words to build up sentences,
  - e.g. 'The fluffy dog is barking loudly'
- using these sentences to build up conversations and narratives or stories, e.g. 'Yesterday there was a fluffy dog in our garden who was barking so loudly that he woke me up!!'
- following the rules of grammar, so that things make sense to other people. This includes:
  - knowing how to put the sentence in the past – 'The fluffy dog **was** barking loudly';
  - or how to indicate there is more than one dog – 'The fluffy dog**s are** barking loudly';
  - or using a pronoun; instead of '**The dog** was barking loudly' – '**He** was barking loudly'.

What is speech?

We often think about 'speech' as giving speeches at a wedding or at a celebration, or even at awards ceremonies, like the Oscars. In fact, speech is the technical term given to the sounds that we use when we are talking.

Saying the right sounds in the right places within words is important. This helps to make sure that people understand what we are saying. It is, though, one of the last skills to be developed in the process of learning to talk. It comes after the ability to understand and use words and sentences.

Speech relies on the ability to process sounds inside our heads, so that we learn which sounds to try and reproduce when we are copying a new word. Children also need to learn how words can be split up across a sentence: unlike when words are written down, when words are spoken, there are no gaps between the different words.

We also need to be able to speak fluently, without too many hesitations or repetitions of words or parts of words.

Getting speech sounds wrong has a big impact on whether someone understands what we are saying: it would be difficult for someone listening to understand the word 'cat' if the sounds were in the wrong order (t-a-c), or if the wrong sounds were used altogether (m-a-k).

Knowing how sounds make up words is also a fundamental skill for reading and writing. Just as a child will learn that the word 'top' is made up of the sounds' t-o-p', they can use this skill later when they want to write this word down.

What is communication?

By 'communication', we aren't thinking, in this context about IT – phones, computers, tablets etc, or even transport links. In this context, we mean the way in which language is used to interact with others;

- Knowing how to use language in different ways:
  - to question: 'Can I have a cake?';
  - to clarify: 'What kind of cake?';
  - to describe: 'The cake with chocolate buttons on top';
  - to debate: 'Yesterday, you told me that there was no more chocolate cake, but I can see it in the packet.'
- Knowing how to use the non-verbal rules of communication:
  - listening well and looking at people when in a conversation;
  - knowing how to talk to others and take turns with listening and speaking;
  - being able to change language to suit the situation or the person being spoken to. (Think of the different ways you might speak to your friend, or your boss, or your grandmother).

A note for you

Throughout the book we will use the term 'talking' to refer to all the different aspects of speech, language (understanding and expressive language) and communication.

The importance of talking, for our children

It is vital that each of these three elements of talking (speech, language and communication) are built up through developing individual skills. If there are difficulties with any one of these elements, what we understand and say, and how we have a conversation, can become confused.

Imagine a situation where only two parts of this 'puzzle' were in place – for example language and communication skills, but not speech sounds. In this example, a person would be able to understand what someone was saying. They would be able to form a response using all the right words and know how to deliver this without making the other person in the conversation feel uncomfortable. However, what the person says would be unclear and difficult to understand. This would mean that, almost immediately, the conversation would break down or dry up.

Or imagine the situation where someone could use all the speech sounds appropriately when they were speaking, but couldn't understand what other people are saying. (You may have experienced this if you have spent any time in another country, even for a short time.) Again, this would lead to significant difficulties for all involved in the conversation.

When we help children to develop the communication skills they need for the rest of their life, we give them the best start. Just as adults are keen to get babies up on their feet and ready to walk, we want our children to be able to ask for things. We want them to tell us what they feel, call us by our names and talk about what their interests are.

Words are incredibly powerful and open up a world of possibilities! We know, through research, that having strong communication skills helps with all subjects at school (including maths and science). It helps children to understand the rules of the classroom, to share and to develop friendships. These skills also help children to understand themselves, to manage their feelings and have strong mental health and wellbeing. Additionally, communication skills help in looking for and finding the jobs that will provide security for our children as adults.

Some children may find learning to talk more difficult. Around 10% of children will continue to experience difficulties with some aspects of talking their whole life. Many more (more than 50% in some areas) start school without the communication skills that they need to learn, make friends and understand what is happening in the classroom.

Did you know?

Talking is a complicated skill.

All children need help to learn to talk. They won't manage it completely on their own.

Knowing how to help children to find their voices is important, from children's youngest years and right into adulthood.

Important adults (parents, grandparents, aunts, uncles and early years practitioners) have a significant role to play in helping children find their voices. The children can't do it without you.

Building brain connections

Everything that you, as an adult, do with a child physically changes the structure of their brain. The words that you say to them (even when they don't yet understand) and the places you take them and the things that you do together build brain connections. This is known as 'neuro-plasticity' and is a fascinating area of research. As a parent or early years practitioner, it is worth knowing this, because it helps you to recognise your specialist role – you are able to change the shape of a baby's brain, a type of early years brain surgeon!

The opposite is also true; the opportunities for learning that a child misses means that the brain connection doesn't happen – not this time, anyway. We can't be educating our babies all of the time, they need time to rest just as we do. However, it is important to know how best to help build your child's brain and what really doesn't help.

While I am on the subject, there is plenty of research that shows that children need a good amount of sleep to help them learn. This applies to babies as much as toddlers and older children. It can be quite hard work being a baby . . . and it can be quite hard work looking after a baby. You are, after all, building the very first foundations of learning.

How do children learn to talk?

The words that come out of a child's mouth are the end-product of lots of learning. The learning starts before birth because babies can actually **hear** from before they are born. Babies hear low frequency noises from 16–18 weeks in the womb. These might be noises such as lawnmowers or cars. From around 24 weeks gestation, babies can start to hear human voices. These voices will be fairly easy for the unborn baby to hear. Particularly the sound of the baby's mum, whose voice they continually hear while in the womb.

Figure 1.2

Many people read books or play music to the baby in the womb. There is lots of research that highlights the benefit of talking to a baby while they are in the womb. This builds up attachment to the baby and gets them used to listening to your voice. It also begins the journey of talking to a child once they are born.

As long as young children's ears, auditory nerves and the part of the brain that processes speech are working, they will be able to hear well. They continue the development of their skills for hearing once they are born. Evidence shows that baby's ears are best tuned to the voices they heard before they were born. There is also evidence that particular tunes that were played when the baby was inside the womb are recognised when children are born. So, babies start to learn to listen to the sounds around them and to pay attention to what they can see and hear.

It should be noted that the ability to 'hear' and the ability to **'listen'** are different things. I'm sure you have had the experience of hearing someone say something, but not knowing what they said because you weren't actively listening. In the same way, we have learnt to 'shut off' noises that are not important to us, the noise of people talking behind us when we are trying to have a conversation on a bus, or the roar of a football field, when we are talking to the person we are sitting next to. Listening is a skill that all children need to learn and we can help by taking away noise that isn't necessary – turning the TV off if no-one is watching it, not having the radio or music playing all the time in the background. We can also help children to know what we want them to be listening to by being at their eye level when we are talking to them and letting them see our faces.

Top tips

Build children's brain connections by giving them plenty of experiences. Talking to a child is an experience that physically helps build their brains.

Help children to tune into you by switching off distracting background noise. Be at their eye level when you are talking to them.

When children learn to listen well and to pay attention to adults in their environment, they start to show an interest and enjoy games which will help develop positive communication skills. One of these early skills is **turn-taking**. This is where children discover that when they play with sounds (babbling), another sound might come back from the adult they are with. Or when they make a face, a funny face might be made right back at them. These are very early forms of conversation. This turn-taking is sometimes known as 'serve and return', like someone hitting a table-tennis ball and having it sent back to them. Have you ever seen what happens when you smile at someone? They will often smile right back.

And did you know that this early turn-taking skill can start straight after birth? There is amazing evidence of a new-born baby working out how to stick their tongue out to their mum or dad who has stuck their tongue out at the baby. It seems as though babies are hard-wired to communicate and we need to give them every opportunity.

From the day they're born, children love playing games and most babies are fascinated by faces and voices. In fact, playing with people is one of the games that children love most. So, what could be more satisfying than sharing fun time with young children, knowing that it's also helping them to develop important skills?

Communication is two-way. It needs to be responded to and reinforced, otherwise communication attempts are just that – attempts with no results. If a baby doesn't get any results from their communication, they will initially increase their attempts, but ultimately give up. Responding to a child's attempts to communicate builds the connections in their brain and helps them recognise what words are. When the child sees a ball and hears the word 'ball', they learn to understand what the word means.

Around the same time as linking words with sounds, babies start to **predict** what is likely to happen next in a situation. These situations might be seeing a familiar adult come into the room or having a mobile wound up ready for 'sleep-time'. As children connect what they see with what they hear, they link words with a particular thing or situation. So, you will see the child getting excited when they hear 'Here's mummy' or 'Do you want some milk?'

Top tips

Babies love repetition – it's how they learn.

Hearing the same word every time they see an object or watch an action will help the baby to learn to connect the word with what it means.

Use the same language every time you change a nappy, get ready for a meal, prepare to go out or help the toddler to go to sleep.

Once children **know what words mean,** they can start to use them. This happens one word at a time to start with – that's all they can pick out of the long sentences they often hear around them. The words may simply be a consistent set of sounds to mean a particular thing. From this point of view, **early words** include sets of sounds such as 'uh-oh', or 'miaow' or 'baa'. We know what the child means, even if this is not the kind of word that an adult would use in their adult conversation.

Right now, even words that are a child's attempt at an adult's words won't sound much like the adult version. Getting the words to be accurate is a later skill. It starts to happen once children build up their knowledge of words and start to use short, then longer sentences.

At this age, there can be plenty of repetition when talking with the child. For example, 'Wow, a dog! Lovely dog. Hello dog. Can you see the dog?' Watch how the child responds to what you say, so that you can interpret what seems to be going on inside their head and speak it out loud, e.g. 'You like that dog' or 'He's looking at you.'

Nursery rhymes and simple, repetitive games, such as peep-bo, will also help the child to listen to you and to learn the words that you're speaking or singing. (See Chapter Four on how music helps language development).

This is the perfect time to introduce the child to books, if you haven't done that already. (See the section on sharing books with a child in Chapter Two). Remember, you don't have to read the story. Just look at the pictures together and talk about what you see.

It is great to get into good habits of spending time in the to and fro of early conversation while the child is very young. This builds attachment and also key communication skills. Watch the child to find out what they are interested in and follow their lead. Remember that everything that you do with them in early childhood builds their brains.

Handy hints

- Build the child's brain by watching what they are interested in and talking about what they see.

- Respond to attempts to communicate by interpreting what you think they are trying to say.

- At the one-word stage (usually around one year old), help support the child to learn words by speaking to them in very short sentences.

- Talk about what you see in front of you, using only one or two words at a time.

- Help build the child's communication skills by giving them plenty of time to 'talk' to you, in whatever way they can.

- When the child attempts to say something, reinforce what they are saying by interpreting their gurgles or saying what you think they mean. This helps the child to hear the word that they are trying to make and supports them to get closer to producing the word more accurately next time.

Milestones guide

We know that children learn to talk in generally the same way, whether they are from Poland, New Zealand, China or Brazil.

There may be some minor variations in how children reach their development targets, but essentially, predicted milestones apply to the majority of children and young people. These milestones provide a guide for whether a child is developing their communication skills in line with expectations for their age, or whether they are late in their development.

Handy hint

In the same way that the 'terrible twos' don't begin immediately after the second birthday, the first word doesn't come out of a child's mouth immediately they have turned one year old.

However, it is a good guide to think of first words being produced around the same time as the child's first birthday. This is often around the time that the child is taking their first steps too.

First words, first steps, first birthday.

It is important that adults working with children know what to expect at different stages of children's development. Some key milestones include:

Before birth: – Babies are developing all the parts of their body that will help them learn to communicate. Babies before birth can hear voices around them (from 24 weeks gestation).

Birth to three months: – Babies turn towards a familiar sound, try to copy facial expressions and recognise familiar voices.

By six months: – Babies make vocal sounds to gain attention and laugh during play. They will also start to play with sounds, babbling to themselves

By nine months: – Children generally learn what individual words mean over their first year and by nine months, they can understand words like 'milk', 'bye', 'up'.

Around 12 months: – Children first use consistent sets of sounds with meaning at around twelve months old. As long as the sounds are used consistently to mean something, we can call this a child's first words, e.g. 'ma' for 'mummy', 'bambap' for 'Grandpap', or 'Yeye' for 'Stephanie'.

12–18 months: – Children's understanding of words and sentences is slightly ahead of their use of words, so while they are using single words, they will understand two key words in a sentence, e.g. they may point when asked 'Where are **teddy's eyes?**' or '**Daddy's ears'.**

Around 18 months: – When children have about 100 single words in their vocabulary, they will start to join words together – at this point, the child's attempts at words can still be quite difficult to understand.

Around two and a half: – Children's understanding remains ahead of their use of words in sentences (using around two to four words together). Around the age of two and a half, children may also start to understand descriptions such as 'big', 'small' and some colour names.

Two and a half to three years: – Soon after children have learnt what words mean, they will start to use them and many children who are two and a half to three years old will use sentences that are over four words long.

Nearly three years: – It isn't until nearer three years of age, that children learn what specific parts of the sentences such as 'in, 'on' and 'under' mean. Most three-year-olds will have a vocabulary size of around 300 words and use sentences of four or five words.

By four years old: – Many children can have mini conversations with adults and children of their own age or older. By this age, it is usual for children to be able to make themselves understood by adults who know them less well.

By five years old: – Children who are developing as expected will have a whole range of skills that will enable them to join in classroom conversations and learn subject vocabulary (such as 'tambourine'). They will be able to follow classroom instructions given to them individually or as part of a whole group.

There are lots of resources available to help understand the milestones usually expected at different ages in the early years. The communication charity, I CAN has a 'Talking Point' website[4] which has a range of information about children's communication development. This includes what to expect when and a progress checker to see if your child is on track with their development. Birth to 5 Matters has also produced non-statutory guidance for early years practitioners which describes the different stages of communication and language development.[5]

To watch a fascinating video sequence about the ages and stages of communication development, visit www.youtube.com/watch?v=jt7y1IM2jOM

A child starting to appear very delayed in their development might be a cause for concern and help can be sought. This help might be in the form of an assessment from a specialist, or guidance for activities to support better language development. Or it might be that parents are asked to change the way that they communicate with their child to make it easier for the child to learn to talk (see Chapter Two).

Key points from this chapter

- Children's communication skills help them to learn, make friends and be successful.

- Talking is made up of skills of understanding, speaking, speech sounds and communication.

- Children learn to talk by being spoken to. This also builds important brain connections.

- There is a sequence to learning to talk which applies to all children.

Notes

1 Field, F (2010) *The Foundation Years: Preventing poor children becoming poor adults. The report of the independent review on poverty and life chances.* The Cabinet Office

2 Allen, G (2011) *Early Intervention: The next steps*. The Cabinet Office

3 Tickell, Dame C (2011) *The Early Years: Foundations for life, health and learning. An Independent Report on the Early Years Foundation Stage to Her Majesty's Government*

4 https://ican.org.uk/i-cans-talking-point

5 https://www.birthto5matters.org.uk/learning-development/ranges/; https://pathways.org/growth-development/2-3-years/videos/

Chapter two

BABY STEPS AND FIRST WORDS – HOW CAN I HELP?

In this chapter you will learn:

- Why it's important that children hear talking before they can talk themselves

- What are interactive behaviours?

- The impact of speaking other languages

- What is 'Parentese'?

- What you can do to help a child to find their voice

  - Following the child's interest

  - Responding to attempts to communicate

  - Feeling comfortable with silence / Pause for the child to respond

  - Making conversation natural

  - Sharing books together

  - Getting their attention first

  - Talking in short simple sentences

  - Repetition

  - Avoiding correcting a child's pronunciation or immature language.

The information that follows applies to babies, toddlers and pre-school children. The ideas can be adapted according to the child's level of development. Examples are given, in each section, of how to do this.

DOI: 10.4324/9781003242840-3

Should I really be talking to a baby before they can talk back to me?

As communication is the foundation for just about every aspect of a child's development, helping build good speech and language skills is one of the most important things you can do.

Children will only learn to talk if they are spoken to at the level that they understand and in a way that is interesting and engaging. This can happen through everyday routines and the care provided for young babies and children.

When it comes to learning communication skills, talking to a child while they are being fed, settled down for a nap, watching what is around them, or when they have just woken up, is just as important as activities with toddlers and pre-school children. We know that learning to talk relies on key underlying skills and these can be supported right from birth (and even before!).

Every child can benefit from activities focusing on communication, whether they are newborn babies or children ready to start school. Talking activities are useful regardless of the child's starting point. They can help those who are a little behind to catch up. They are also useful for helping those who are developing well to build even stronger foundations.

Most children have an automatic interest in voices and faces and they will start by learning to focus on sounds and to copy some of what they see and hear. Some adults may feel self-conscious if they are not used to talking with people who don't talk back. It's something that many adults get used to very easily – look at the number of adults who will happily talk to a pet, without getting any verbal response!

Ideas of things to chat about include talking about what the child can see. Shared interest develops from about eight months old. This is where a child will look at what you are looking at. At this age, the child might also encourage you to look at what they are interested in, by pointing to it.

With very young children, talk about what they are experiencing, e.g. 'Ooh, you like that.'; 'Is that your hand? Shall we wash your hand?'; 'That food was lovely – yummy dinner.'

Make sure to leave plenty of time to respond to any gurgles or babbles that you hear. This is the start of early conversations with the child and lets them know that you are interested in what they are saying, even if it doesn't make much sense yet.

New research carried out on behalf of the Departments of Health and Social Care and the Department for Education[1] has identified key behaviours used by adults which support children learning to talk. These behaviours are all focused around responding to children in order to support their communication development. Some may seem obvious and some less so.

Figure 2.1

We learn how adults talk with children by observing other adults doing the same. In some cases, we might have to adjust what we do because the people who we learnt from hadn't learnt the most useful behaviours.

The key 'interactive behaviours' that are now being discussed with new parents by health visitors in England are described below. The research goes on to identify when these interactive behaviours can be used. It is no surprise that they can be used at any time. It is really helpful if you build them into your everyday routine, at times such as:

- bathtime

- mealtimes

- out and about

- bedtime

- at the shops

- sharing books

- at toddler group

- playing with toys

- any other 'together time'.

Tips for interactive behaviours

- Get down to the child's level, or bring them up to yours.

- Follow the child's lead and interests.

- Pause and watch the child to see what they are interested in.

- Listen, watch and respond to their communication – this can be words, pointing, sounds or movements.

- Describe what the child is doing or looking at. Imagine what they are thinking and feeling and say that.

- Show them you are having fun by using an interesting voice.

- If they do communicate, copy what they say (or mean to say) and add a word.

- Use fewer questions. Instead, describe what is happening.

- When you do ask questions, try to keep them open – 'Where…?', 'Who …?' (for younger children) and 'When…?' and 'Why…?' (for older children), rather than questions that lead to a 'yes' or 'no' answer, e.g. 'Are you helping teddy?'.

Make talking part of everything that you do with children. This provides the best opportunity for children to learn vital communication skills. The majority of these useful interactive behaviours will be discussed in more detail in later parts of this guide.

Speaking other languages

The most important skill that a child can learn is how to communicate. This applies whatever language is spoken at home.

What children need is a strong foundation in their home language. They can learn other languages, including English, later when they need it. In fact, it will be easier to learn other languages if the child's home language is strong. This way, children will have a framework of words to map other words onto.

The advice given to parents is always to talk in the language that you know best. If that isn't English, use your home language. This provides the best model for the child to copy and they can learn English from a native English speaker when they get to nursery or school.

If you work in a school or early years setting, you will need to talk in the language of that location. However, if you speak another language naturally and there are children in the school or setting who speak the same language, you can help by talking in the language that you both understand. This won't harm a child's communication development (and may well help if they already hear that language at home).

Do check with the school or setting managers and the child's parents which language they would prefer you to use in the school or setting.

All of the tips about speaking in short sentences, giving the child plenty of time to respond, talking about what you see in front of you and interpreting the child's communication attempts apply to the home language, as well as to English.

Top tips

If you are a parent, speak to your child in the language that you feel most comfortable with.

All of the tips about how to build communication skills still apply in your home language.

If you work with children, check which language is appropriate to use in that setting and with different children.

Speaking more than one language is a benefit and has been shown to have other positive impacts on intelligence. Children learning more than one language (as happens in 75% of the world) are no more likely to have a difficulty in talking or understanding than they would if they spoke only one language.

If you are working with a child who speaks another language at home, it is important to find out how they are communicating in this language, rather than looking only at English. This will help you to see how their English is developing, compared with their home language. (Children who have speech, language and communication needs will demonstrate difficulties in all of the languages that they understand and use.)

They'll talk when they're ready won't they?

As a speech and language therapist, I have heard many times parents say that they were told that Einstein didn't talk in full sentences until he was five 'and he did OK, didn't he?'.

There is no conclusive proof about whether Einstein was or wasn't a late talker, but there has been a significant amount of research about the impact of late communication development. This comes from a wide range of researchers. These impacts range from difficulties at school, struggling to build relationships, impacts on self-esteem and for some children and

Figure 2.2

young people, behaviour difficulties and getting into trouble with the law. That doesn't mean every child who is a late talker will run into these difficulties later in life. We do know that good early communication skills are a protective factor in positive life chances.

Research shows....

Children's vocabulary at age five is the best predictor of whether children who experienced social disadvantage in childhood were able to 'buck the trend' and escape poverty in later adult life.

Strong early speech and language skills were seen to lead to positive life outcomes. This is the basis for significant investment from the Department for Education and Public Health England.

'Parentese'

There has been much research into 'Parentese' – the way that parents communicate with their children when the children are in the early stages of learning to talk. (This was originally known as 'Motherese' in the 1960s. Since then, it has been recognised that both parents use this way of talking to help children's early language development.)

Parentese is a sing-song way of talking with more exaggerated intonation, often with a lot of repetition and increased stress on particular words. Children and babies love this way of being spoken to and often reward the speaker with smiles, gurgles and increased interaction.

Parentese comes naturally to many adults. According to Nicole Overy (Kids Place West's Speech-Language Pathologist)[2], adults often have concerns that Parentese can sound silly or obnoxious. Nicole states that, in fact, 'research has shown that there is true value to Parentese' – it helps support a child's language development.

Stephen Malloch and Colwyn Tervarthen's book[3] highlights that babies' and young children's hearing is most tuned to middle C on the musical scale. In studies on the 'Parentese' used by both males and females, a significantly greater proportion of the sentences are focused around middle C. This is unlikely to be a coincidence. Fundamentally, we know what babies and young children need and our natural tendency is to provide it through Parentese.

The difference between some baby-talk and Parentese is that in Parentese, adult words are used. Whereas in some baby-talk, words can become less intelligible, rather than more intelligible, e.g. Baby-talk: 'oo's a lovely, wovely, dovely likkle baba den?'; Parentese: 'Hello! You're so gorgeous!'

In spoken sentences, unlike written sentences, there are no gaps between words. So, the child has to work out which individual words to listen to in the apparent jumble of sounds that are spoken sentences. Extending the vowels, slowing speech down and using plenty of repetition helps children to know where one word ends and another begins. This way of talking is often used to emphasise key words relating to what is in front of the child, e.g. 'Wow, a ball. Bouncy, bouncy, bouncy ball.'

Did you know?

The varied intonation and sing-song approach found in 'Parentese' is more interesting to children and babies than most adult conversation. It indicates to a child that they, in particular, are being spoken to.

This helps to draw children's attention to what the adult is saying and is vital for supporting early language development.

Interestingly, it's not only parents who instinctively talk to children in this way, but also older siblings and other older children. At some point, many people may become very aware of how different this 'Parentese' sounds and try to make it more like normal adult conversation. By doing this, they are inadvertently making it harder for children to be interested in what is being said and to understand it.

Helping children learn to talk

Following the child's interest

Noticing what a child is interested in or looking at, and talking with the child about that, is known as 'contingent talk'. This has recently been found (by Dr Matthews and Professor Pine[4]) to be one of the most important ways to support a child's communication development.

Following the child's interest helps children to match the word that they are hearing with the object, person, action or concept in front of them – making it much easier to learn the words. Contingent talk is based on a child's interests and we all know that we learn much more about what we are interested in, than something that we are not really paying attention to.

When we're talking about something that is in front of a child, that they are showing an interest in, we tend to repeat the key word over and over again. For example, 'look at that cat. What a lovely cat. Hello cat – how are you?' (when a child has no or few individual words). The child's attention is already directed to what we are talking about and this makes it easier for them to learn the words (in this case, 'cat').

Noticing what a child is interested in also helps us tune into their attempts to communicate. This means that we can respond, reinforce and model the adult version of the word the child is trying to say.

When, as a speech and language therapist, I need to 'translate what a child is saying' I always try to get clues from what they are looking at or playing with at the time. As parents or early years practitioners, we need to do the same: It once took me a very long time to work out what my son was saying when he was talking about a 'bakey bus' until I focused on the fact that we were walking past a holly hedge when he said these words. Eventually, I understood that he was talking about a 'spikey bush'.

Dr Matthews and Professor Pine are so focused on contingent talk that they set up an intervention to support parents to learn how to do this better. They videoed new parents interacting with their children and watched the videos with the new parents, to help the parents to notice what their children were interested in; to recognise when their child babbled or gestured; and to comment on what their child could see. The parents were then asked to practice noticing these aspects of their children's interaction for 15 minutes every day for a month. After a month, it was identified that these parents were more likely to talk to their child in this contingent way, than parents who had not taken part in the intervention. Interestingly, there was also found to be a positive impact on the toddlers' ability to learn new words. It was also identified that this technique needs to remain being used in order to continue to positively impact on children's language development.

Responding to attempts to communicate

From the moment babies are born, they are interested in key aspects of communication – faces, noises, copying. There are some fascinating videos on-line that demonstrate how a newborn baby can attempt to copy their parent sticking out their tongue (e.g. https://tinyurl. com/47mj4k4n). Babies appear hard-wired to communicate. Yet, we know that adults have a key role in shaping and supporting this skill.

As babies grow, they make noises that an adult can choose to ignore or respond to. Responding positively to a child's noises generally encourages them to make the noise again and this becomes the very first step in conversation.

When a child shows an interest in something or points to it, or shows how they are feeling (positively or negatively), adults can name what the child is looking at or feeling (for babies, right through to pre-school children). This introduces a word for the item, action or feeling and helps a child to understand what that word means.

Figure 2.3

Each time we respond to a child's attempts to communicate, we help shape their communication – we build on these early skills and teach a child that their communication is important. The Hanen programme[5] encourages parents and caregivers to observe children, wait and listen for their attempts to communicate . . . and then respond. This means that we are communicating with children on their terms, shaping their communication and responding positively.

One of our tasks in supporting communication is to watch what children are already doing to communicate and saying the words that they might use, so that they can do so when they are ready. For example, a toddler raising their arms to be lifted up can be told 'up' when the adult is lifting them. This helps the child to get to know what this word means so that they can use it when they are ready. Another time, the child might lift their arms up and say 'ah'. The adult can again interpret this word as the child's attempt at the word 'up'. The adult can reinforce and help to 'shape' the child's attempt at the word by the adult saying 'up' as the child is lifted up.

It is important that we follow what a child is interested in and trying to communicate with us (as described above), rather than giving them information and naming objects that they aren't interested in, or talking about something that they can't see in front of them.

As children develop communication through gestures and words, they will start to use their communication skills in a range of ways – to request, greet, demand, ask, explain etc. The more we respond positively to these skills, the more we demonstrate that we value communication and the more a child is likely to do it.

Did you know?

Researchers in America in the 1990s[1] counted the number of the same, or different words that were spoken to children in different types of households.

The stunning finding was that, by the age of three years, some groups of children hear 30 million fewer normal, everyday words spoken to them in total, than other groups of children.

In addition, the children who heard fewer words spoken to them tended to have smaller vocabularies. These children also talked later than the children who were involved in more conversations and heard a greater number of words.

Responding to children's attempts to communicate is a great way of making sure that children hear more words and that these words are meaningful to them. When the words relate to what children are interested in, they will be more useful.

Choosing when to talk and when to be quiet

In times past, people talked about 'language-rich environments'. This was the idea that 'flooding' children with words would help them to know what words mean and enable them to use long and complicated sentences.

In fact, as described above, children (of all ages) learn new words best when they are said on their own or in short sentences. This is particularly when the words are used about an object that the child can see in front of them. Or an action that they are doing or can see, or an experience that they are having at that moment.

We also know that children are already communicating before they use their first words. This can be visual – smiling (at 6 weeks or before), pointing (this usually starts by 8 months old), waving, shaking their heads or making faces. Or it could be auditory – blowing raspberries, making animal noises, using sounds like 'uh-oh' to mean 'oh dear' or 'whoops'. We can only recognise this communication if we watch what the child is doing. This often involves us listening (being quiet for a while), rather than talking.

When we do comment on what a child (of any age) can see or is doing, we need to give time for the child to absorb and process what we have said. This allows time for the words to sink in, so that the child can plan their response. It can often be quite hard to do, but it helps children to understand and think about what they have heard. Remembering that we need to be quiet also helps us not to be attempting to 'flood' children with language.

> **Handy hint**
>
> It may take up to ten seconds for a child to respond to what we are saying. So, we need to feel comfortable with waiting for their response, without saying anything else.

Making conversation natural

Naming items that a child is interested in or following their eye gaze and talking about what they are looking at is a natural way to have a conversation. Asking children to name items or talk about particular topics that you, as an adult, have chosen isn't natural. What's more, this type of testing or quizzing children doesn't help them to learn words and to use them in conversations. It adds pressure to talking and might make children feel that they have to perform.

In the same way, if a child pronounces a word in a child-like way, the best way to support them is for you to use the word in an adult way in the conversation. This is described later, under 'Avoiding correcting a child's pronunciation or immature language'.

The most natural type of conversation is one where one person speaks and another responds, and then the first person speaks again. Commenting on what a child is doing or can see, and waiting for their response, is a useful way of doing this. It may take some practice if you are used to asking lots of questions.

Top tip

It is better to say 'Ooh, I can see a cow', than to say 'What's that?'.

In the first example, a child learns to match the animal with the name of the animal. They can then use that word when they are ready, later in the conversation, or at another time.

When asked a question, the child is likely to feel under pressure to perform. This is more likely to stop them from speaking than to encourage easy communication.

Sharing books together

Young babies (as early as the first few weeks of life) enjoy looking at high-contrasting, black and white images with sharp outlines. These are much easier for a very young baby to see, while their eyesight is still developing. You can look together at clearly distinguished black and white images, especially those that resemble faces. This type of stimulation, according to Professor Usha Goswami, director of the Centre for Neuroscience in Education at Cambridge University 'basically gets the system up and running'.

Looking at images together with babies is the start of sharing books and helps babies and young children to gain an interest in pictures and learn how to handle books. Cloth or thick card books mean that adults worry less about the book being damaged and children will learn to appreciate looking at books together with an adult. However, many toddlers and very young children can learn to be careful with pages and enjoy sharing paper books with adults too.

Children might show their interest in a book by holding it or chewing it (if they are very young). You can help them to understand how to use a book by holding it so that they can see it, preferably with the child sitting on your lap, or next to you in a cosy place. Sharing attention on an item or picture can begin as early as eight months of age, though children even younger than this show interest in images.

In this way very, very young children can enjoy books being shared by a parent, carer, adult or older child.

Figure 2.4

You can make the books even more exciting by using exaggerated intonation when describing what's in the pictures or reading the words aloud. The child will love it if you say words in silly voices (pretending to be some of the characters in the book), or lead the child's interest by saying things like 'Oh, look it's a ... . . .' when you turn over a new page.

Top tip

Book-sharing time is a very special time and helps build attachment and joint attention (valuable in supporting early language development).

At an early age (from under one, to two and a half to three years old), it doesn't really matter too much about the story or any words on the page.

Even after this, adults can just talk about the pictures that are on each page. The most important thing is that the child hears the adult talk in short simple sentences about what is in the pictures.

Many of the 'Words Together' books and some other books have a clue on one page about what you can see on the next page (for example the monkey's tail, indicating that you will see Monkey on the next page). Draw the child's attention to specific parts of the picture such as this – it helps to make the book so much more interesting.

Taking time to watch and wait for the child's response about what's on the page, or what you are talking about helps you to know what they're interested in. You can then respond by talking about what the child is looking at. This is all part of the 'serve and return' backwards and forwards interaction that makes up conversations.

Another useful aspect of books (and this fits right into what children love) is that they are repetitive: They sound the same each time they are shared together. This applies even if you're not reading the story – you are very likely to talk about the same things on each page every time you share the book. The repetitive aspect helps children to learn the words that they hear as they relate to the pictures on the page. They also provide a model for children to copy and join in when they are ready.

The University of Sheffield has put together a useful guide for how to share books together.[6] The Book Trust also gives some helpful hints.[7]

The joint attention that sharing a book with a child offers means that the words that you are using when you look at a book with a child relate directly to what you can both see. This means that the child is learning the words for the pictures that you are both looking at, especially when you point to different parts of the picture.

Book sharing is one of the aspects of home life and life in early years settings that has been found to make the most difference to children's language development.[8]

Did you know?

Books like those in the 'Words Together' series help scaffold children's language development – spanning the very important stage of development from individual words to short sentences.

Sharing books provides so much more than language learning opportunities too. When children move on to books with more information in them, they also learn about things that they don't have experience of in their immediate environment. Talking about what is in the book allows the adult a chance to share something of the world around the child and to learn what interests the child and what their views are.

Understanding that the marks on the page stand for words with meaning is a crucial stage in learning to read and write. This unlocks the world for children in terms of education, interests, hobbies, crafts and every aspect of learning and development. The book sharing that you do with a baby or young child sets the foundations for the written information that may change their lives when they are older.

Getting their attention first

Much as it's important to respond to a child's interests and the sounds that they are making, we can also help a child to learn new words by pointing things out to them. It is key to make sure that you have the child's attention first, before you talk to them.

In Chapter One, we discussed the importance of supporting a child's development of listening skills by reducing the background noise that they hear all of the time. This means that it is easier for a child to know what to listen to. We can also help get a child's attention by saying their name, and waiting until they are ready, before we start to speak. Talking to the back of a child's head or talking about one thing when they are focusing on another rarely achieves the results that we want.

When we get a child's attention first, we know that they are listening to us and that what we say has more chance of making sense to them. It is not necessary for a child to look at us when we are speaking (or when they are speaking to us): often people look together at an object or action that is being spoken about – this is known as joint attention.

Handy hint

Gaining a child's attention enables them to concentrate more fully on what you are saying.

Having joint attention (the child's attention being on an object that you are looking at together, or action that you are doing together) helps the child to match what they are hearing to the object or action in front of them.

As with many other skills, children need to learn how to switch their attention from one place to another. They will rely on adults to help them do that, right the way up to school age. Cooper, Moodley and Reynell described the growth of attention skills way back in 1978,[9] pointing out that young children can't be expected to pay attention to anything if they are engaged with another activity. This is why gaining a child's attention before talking to them is so important.

Talking in short, simple sentences

Babies and children develop skills in understanding words before they learn to talk. As they learn to talk, their understanding skills are always slightly ahead of their talking – just as we may understand parts of a language that we learnt at school, although we may not be able to speak so much of that language.

Figure 2.5

To start with, children will only understand a few key words in the sentences that they hear – usually one to two key words up until the age of one, two to three key words between one and two. After this, the number of words and complexity of vocabulary increases. For this reason, it is important to use short sentences with children so that they don't have to pick out the key words from a much longer sentence. Saying things like 'bed-time', or 'look, a bus' is much more effective for toddlers and very young children, than saying much longer sentences. It also means that the child has much more chance of understanding what is being said to them – making communication more effective.

Sometimes, adults can be reluctant to use simple sentences because adding in lots of words can make the sentence sound friendlier. For example, compare 'tidy-up time' (two words) with 'Come along now, it's time to tidy up so that we can go outside to play' (16 words). It is worth recognising, however, that using a long sentence reduces the likelihood of a child understanding it. This, in fact, makes the sentence less friendly for that child. This applies to children right the way up to their pre-school year and beyond.

The advantage of using short sentences is also that it provides a model for a child to follow when they are ready. A two-year-old is much more likely to be able to use the phrase 'tidy-up time' in their conversations, than the alternative 16-word sentence given above. Short sentences work to help both the child's understanding and their expressive language skills.

Top tip

When talking with a child, use one word more than they generally use.

If a child tends to use two-word sentences, use three-word sentences with that child, e.g. Child: 'Big bus', Adult: 'Yes – big bus driving.'

This is sometimes known as 'match plus one'.

Repetition

Anyone who has spent any time around young children knows that they like to do the same thing over, and over again. Whether it is putting a spoon in a cup and taking it out again, putting it in again and taking it out again, or playing a tickling game, or hearing the same story over, and over again. It seems that children have an in-built sense of what helps them learn and repetition is one of these aspects.

It has been said that children need to hear a word 500 times before they can use it. This probably applies to the first 50–75 words that a child uses and after that, they may need to hear new words fewer than 500 times: by the time a child gets to school, the research suggests that a word only needs to be heard 17 times before it is added to a child's vocabulary. However, our focus here is very young children, so the need for repetition is likely to be higher.

Repetition in everyday conversation provides more than one opportunity for a child to hear a certain word. It means that the word can be heard in lots of different ways, in different parts of the sentence and in different contexts. For example, a child looking at a dog might hear the adult say 'Look, a dog . . .The dog's jumping . . . Lovely dog . . . Bye-bye dog.'

Scientists have found that hearing repetition of words in context with young children improves their language development even 18 months later. Rochelle Newman, professor and chair of UMD's Department of Hearing and Speech Sciences reported 'Parents who repeat words more often to their infants have children with better language skills a year and a half later.'[1]

Top tip

Make opportunities for the same words to be heard over again by children. It helps them to learn the word meanings and children have a very high boredom threshold.

Repetition really does help them learn to talk. You may then hear the child using the same words that you regularly use at nappy changing time, when going out or putting toys away.

Avoiding correcting a child's pronunciation or immature language

It is important to make conversation natural, so avoid asking a child to repeat your words or asking them to say something in a certain way. The only thing achieved by asking a child to repeat your words is enabling them to copy what you say at that particular time: it doesn't help in changing the way that they talk going forwards. In fact, a request for a child to copy an adult exactly may increase the pressure on the child. It can make them too aware of how they are speaking and reduce their interest in talking.

All children will use child-like ways of pronouncing words or saying sentences, because words and sentences are very complicated and these complex skills can't be learnt straight away. When they make child-like simplifications, the best way to respond is with the adult version of the word or sentence. The child will take this in and be able to use it later, when they are ready. For example, if a child says 'gaggy' instead of 'daddy', say 'Yes, it's daddy'. Or if they say 'Budding tee' when you get the toothbrush out, you can say 'We're brushing teeth.'

Key points from this chapter

Children need responsive adults to help them to learn to talk.

Children with strong early language skills have the most positive life outcomes.

Speaking to children in the language you (and they) know best is important.

Adults adopt useful simplified ways of talking with children that encourages children to be interested in what they are saying. This is known as 'Parentese'.

There are key 'interactive behaviours' that we can use to help children learn to understand what we say and to talk for themselves.

Notes

1 Departments of Health and Social Care and the Department for Education (2020) *Early Language Identification Measure and Intervention: Guidance handbook: To support children's speech, language, and communication development as part of the 2 to 2½ year review in England*

2 Overy, N (2017) *Parentese: What is it and why you should do it.* AZOPT Kids Place. https://azopt.net/parentese/

3 Malloch, S and Trevarthen, C (eds) (2009) *Communicative Musicality: Exploring the basis of human companionship.* OUP

4 https://www.sheffield.ac.uk/polopoly_fs/1.731434!/file/NurseryWorld.pdf

5 www.hanen.org

6 www.lucid.ac.uk/media/2004/enjoying-reading-with-your-child-a-guide-for-parents.pdf

7 https://www.booktrust.org.uk/books-and-reading/tips-and-advice/reading-tips

8 Millenium cohort study; https://wordsforlife.org.uk/activities/sharing-stories-together/

9 Cooper, J, Moodley, M and Reynell, J (1978) *Helping Language Development: A developmental programme for children with early language handicaps.* Hodder Arnold

Chapter three

THE IMPORTANT TWO-WORD STAGE

The step from single words to short and then longer sentences, necessarily goes through the important two-word stage. This usually happens around 18 months, but some children really struggle to understand that it is possible to link two concepts together in one short sentence.

In this chapter, you will learn about:

- Pivot words

- Activities and games that support children to join words together:

  - Tidying up

  - Going to sleep

  - Make your own slide

  - Posting toys

  - Bathtime

  - Action words

  - Asking for more

  - The 'Words Together' series of books.

Pivot words

Most children learn the same first words – 'mummy', 'daddy', 'ball', 'teddy', 'bye', 'up', 'more' and the names of the key people in their family.

DOI: 10.4324/9781003242840-4

There are two reasons for this – one is that these words are used over and over again in many households and early years settings up and down the country. The other is that many of these words have the sounds in them that are easiest for young children to say. These are the sounds that are formed at the front of the mouth, where children can see to copy most easily and where there is the greatest sensitivity. In fact, in nearly all languages, the words for the male and female parent are words that use sounds from the front of the mouth, e.g. 'mamma' and 'babbo' in Italian, 'mammy' and 'deddy' in Gujurati, 'mamia' and 'tatus' in Polish etc.

Some early language development programmes use these early words as a simple check to see how children are developing. The Early Language Identification Measure introduced by Public Health England to support the Healthy Child Programme development review uses a word checklist and Ann Locke created a list of the first hundred words in her Teaching Talking programme.[1] Obviously, there is a degree of variation from family to family – for example my son's first word was 'Bramble' – the name of our naughty puppy. My brother's first word was 'tractor' because, at that time, a tractor drove past the end of our road every day.

Once children have learnt to understand and use approximately 100 words (usually by around 18 months), they will start to join words together. This is an important stage in language development as it marks the start of word combinations that lead to sentences. Ultimately, these short sentences then lead to longer conversations.

In the initial stages of combining words, the same two words can be used to have a range of meanings. For example, 'mummy sock' can mean 'mummy, here's my sock'; 'mummy, this is your sock'; 'where is mummy's sock?'; 'where is my sock, mummy?' etc. In these early stages, it is the context that will help us to understand what children mean.

Did you know?

When children join words together to make short sentences, they often use particular words (known as 'pivot words') to do this.

Pivot words are those that can easily have another word added onto them, making a short sentence. For example, 'bye-bye' can have another number of different words added to it to make a sentence – 'bye-bye baby', 'bye-bye teddy', 'bye-bye car' etc. Also 'away' can be combined with different words when tidying up, e.g. 'tractor away', 'cat away', 'monkey away' etc.

So, pivot words can either be the first or the second word in a two-word sentence. The key is that they can have a range of alternative words joining with them to create meaning.

Figure 3.1

Some children have particular difficulties moving from the one-word stage to joining words together. It is only by going through this two-word stage that children can use language to describe, explain, question, direct, expand and all of the other key uses of communication.

The 'Words Together' resources help children to learn to join words together by using pivot words. Our simple picture books are aimed at children at this very important stage in their development, no matter how old they are.

You can also play games to help children learn how words go together. This chapter has lots of examples of how you can help develop these fundamental skills.

Games you can play

Children learn from what they hear around them (when you have their attention and they have learnt to listen) and what they see in front of them.

When the individual child knows and uses around 100 words, they are ready to start joining words together. They will start with 'pivot words' as described above.

You can help by playing fun and repetitive games that use the same sentence structure over and over again to help the child learn how words join together. You can build these games into your daily routine and use a sing-song tone when you say the two words together, e.g. 'Bye-bye teddy', 'Bye-bye ball', 'Bye-bye cup' etc.

Children hearing adults use two-word phrases frequently are more likely to copy this sentence structure. These games are about providing an opportunity for the child to hear simple sentence structures that they can move towards including in their own talking.

Tidying up

It's good to get into the habit of putting one set of toys away with a child before they get the next set out. As well as helping to keep the space a bit tidier, it helps the child to be able to concentrate on one set of toys. It means that they are less distracted by all the other toys that they have been playing with so far that day.

When you are tidying up together, use the pivot word 'away' to attach to a range of other words and repeat this each time you put a toy in the box or bag. So, when you are tidying up farm animals, you can say 'Pig away' . . . 'Cow away' . . . 'Dog away' . . . 'Horse away' . . . 'Sheep away' etc.

Make sure you leave plenty of pauses in between each two-word phrase so that the child has an opportunity to copy it when they are ready.

The child might even join in with the second part of the phrase, if this is the stage that they are at. If a child does say one of the two parts of the sentence, repeat the sentence back to them using both words, e.g. Child: 'Cat', Adult: 'Cat away'.

Going to sleep

Having a bedtime routine is important in preparing a child for sleeping and is likely to end in a better night's sleep for you all. Research says that giving a child a bath, brushing their teeth and having some quiet time (without screens) such as looking at a book together is a great way of preparing a child for bed. The US Department of Health and Human Sciences in association with the Head Start programme calls this routine 'Brush, book, bed'.

When settling a child down to sleep, try saying goodnight to the range of toys in the room, e.g. 'Night-night teddy', 'Night-night dog', 'Night-night Baby', 'Night-night tiger' etc. You can even say 'Night-night everyone' as you close the curtains or blind with the child.

Children love this type of routine and, because you are doing this every night, the child will have plenty of chance to hear the two-word sentences that you are using. The child can then join in when they are ready.

In the day-time, you could play games with the same phrases pretending to put the child's toys to bed by covering them up with blankets.

Make your own slide

Toys don't need to be expensive to be great fun: cardboard tubes can make a great slide and a fun way to play with toys popping out at the bottom of the tube. You can make your own toy slide and talk about the toys that are going down it.

There is also an element of surprise that is available when using a cardboard tube as it's not always predictable when the toy will come out of the bottom of the 'slide'. You can control this to a certain extent by tipping the tube at a greater or lesser angle to slow down or speed up the toy travelling down.

Use pivot word sentences like 'Ball down', 'Whale down', 'Horse down', 'Cup down'. You could also add 'Where's the horse?' 'Horse there', to provide some excitement. Remember though, that children love repetition, and it is the repetition and the same sentence structure with the pivot words that helps the child to learn how to join words together.

When you're outside, you can use these same sentences on a real child's slide. Remember that the sing-song tone that you use will help to focus the child on the words that you are using (see notes on 'Parentese' in Chapter Two).

Figure 3.2

Posting toys

A posting game is another game that uses a cardboard box. Cut a hole in the front or the lid of the box so that you can post toys into it and then get them out later. The hole will need to be the right size for your choice of toys.

Choose toys that the child knows the names for and post them one at a time into the cardboard box. Each time the toy disappears, say the toy's name with the pivot word 'gone', e.g. 'Car gone', 'Bus gone', 'Plane gone' etc.

An exciting voice, a sing-song tone and lots of facial expression will help this game to be even more fun. The child may well want to post toys too and you can slow this down by putting your hand across the hole until you have commented on the previous toy.

Remember to leave plenty of time for the child to comment back about what's happening. This game is about developing communication skills, not posting skills! If the child uses one of the two words that you are modelling for them, repeat the full two-word sentence back, e.g. Child: 'Car'. Adult: 'Car gone'.

Bathtime

If you are looking after a child at home, or you are playing in water in an early years setting, you can talk about washing different toys or parts of the body. The pivot word in this game is 'wash'. Use two-word sentences such as 'Wash nose', 'Wash ears', 'Wash toes' or 'Wash duck', 'Wash elephant', 'Wash monkey' (naming familiar toys that the child is playing with in the water).

Because bathtime is often a daily routine, this provides plenty of opportunity for the child to hear the same two-word phrases multiple times. This will help them to use these sentences when they are ready.

Action words

Children usually hear and use names of objects, people and places first. However, it is important that they also learn words for actions. All adult sentences have an action word in them, so this is an important step for a child.

When playing together with a child, use the action word as a pivot word and make all the toys do the same thing, e.g. 'Teddy's sleeping', 'Dog's sleeping', 'Monkey's sleeping' 'Rabbit's sleeping.' etc.

Early action words that are commonly used by children include 'jumping', 'eating', 'sitting', 'crying' or 'walking'.

Asking for more

'More' is one of the earliest pivot words and is best used when the child is eating. It is easy to link 'more' to any item of food or drink and comment when a child is eating. You could also use 'more' during games that the child is very excited by, e.g. blowing bubbles. Remember to make two-word sentences such as 'More bubbles'; 'More peas'; 'More juice'; 'More milk' etc. or even 'More breakfast'; 'More dinner'.

As always, using a sing-song voice and waiting for the child to respond is important in supporting them to move onto using two words together when they are ready.

If a child says 'more' to indicate that they want more, you can encourage them to use two words by offering a choice of items, e.g. 'More milk or more juice?'. It is important to use both the pivot word and the item in the choices that you give, as you are providing the model of the sentence that you want the child to use. For example, if you said 'Do you want more milk or juice?', the child is likely to respond with only one word, i.e. 'Milk' or 'Juice'. Whereas if you say 'Do you want more milk or more juice?', the child is more likely to use both words, 'More juice', in their reply.

The 'Words Together' series of books

This series of books, also published by Routledge, has been especially designed to support children to understand and use two-word sentences. This is in recognition of the important leap in language development that two-word sentences offer.

Each book is based around one pivot word, providing the opportunity for the child to hear the same sentence structure all the way through the book. The books build on repetition and have engaging illustrations that draw children into the world of the toddler in the book. Because the toddler in the book is anonymous, the child sharing the book with an adult can imagine that they are doing what the toddler is doing.

The books are based around everyday routines and activities – the type that any child may regularly be involved with.

When sharing the books with the child, use the tone of your voice to talk in an excited way about the pictures. Read aloud the two-word sentences that are written on each page of the book. Talk about the pictures together and you will find that the child joins in with the words when they are ready.

Key points from this chapter

Once children have around 100 individual words (usually around 18 months old), they may start to join words together.

This is an important step in moving from naming individual items or actions to using sentences and then having conversations.

'Pivot words' play an important role in supporting children to move onto using two-word sentences, whatever their age.

> There are a range of games that adults can play with children to help build these skills.
>
> The 'Words Together' series of books focuses particularly on this stage of development.

Note

1 Ann Locke, *First 100 Words* (Speech and Language Therapy Advice Sheets), https://view.officeapps. live.com/op/view.aspx?src=https%3A%2F%2Fwww.gwh.nhs.uk%2Fmedia%2F141128%2 Fthe_ first_100_words.doc

Chapter four

OTHER THINGS TO THINK ABOUT

In this chapter, we will think about

- Hearing difficulties

- How to interpret what children are telling us

- When to use dummies and when to stop

- Whether children benefit from screen time

- What toys children might need

- Whether baby-signing is useful.

Hearing difficulties

Learning to listen is the fundamental first step in learning to understand and to speak (see Chapter One). Difficulties with hearing will affect the child's ability to listen.

Newborn hearing screening is offered to all babies in England, ideally within the first four to five weeks after they are born. (Other countries will have different programmes of hearing checks). There are regular checks on children's hearing carried out by health visitors and school nurses in the pre-school and early school years.

Frequent colds can affect children's (and adults') hearing. This may mean that some children have intermittent hearing difficulties that may be missed by the regular hearing checks. These intermittent hearing difficulties are caused by fluid collecting in the (usually empty) middle part of the ear, reducing the flow of soundwaves in the ear. This is sometimes known as 'glue ear'.[1] If a child has a delay in their language development, it is important to ensure

DOI: 10.4324/9781003242840-5

that their hearing is checked. (You can check whether a child's language is delayed by referring to the milestones guide in Chapter One.) Also, note down how often the child has a cold so that you can work out the possible impact on their hearing.

Children who have persistent colds that affect their hearing, impacting on their language development, may benefit from a simple operation to provide 'grommets'. These are tiny tubes which are placed in a hole in the eardrum. They let air get in and out of the ear and help to keep the ear healthy and clear from the fluid which can cause hearing problems.[2]

How do I know what they mean?

I remember when I was first a parent, being told that I would get used to my babies' cries and start to know what they mean. I never did get to know what the different cries meant. Even after my third child, it was a guessing game. Were they hungry, uncomfortable, in need of a nappy change? I just had to go through all the options and try to work out what worked in helping them to feel more settled.

The weeks turned into months and I was getting used to parenthood. Then I was able to see, by my babies' faces and their body language, what interested them, what surprised them and what they didn't like so much. We grew in our understanding together: I knew that it was important to 'reflect back' what my child appeared to be saying, even though they were using sounds, movement and facial expressions only. We started to have mini conversations which went something like this:

PARENT: Hello. How are you today?

BABY: Wriggle, grin, gurgle

PARENT: You're feeling OK? Well that's good. You like days like this?

BABY: Wriggle, mouth open, gurgle

PARENT: But there's something you want to say?

BABY: Fidget, gurgle, eyes widen

PARENT: Yes?

BABY: Wriggle, gurgle, grin

PARENT: Well that's interesting!

BABY: Wriggle, fidget, gurgle, gurgle....[3]

Sometimes, I could see that my baby was interested in something in particular. At that point, I would name the item that they were looking at and, if possible, bring it closer for my baby to explore. During their exploration, I would repeat the word for the object or action that they were interested in lots of times. For example, 'Wow, a teddy . . . Look at that teddy . . . You like the teddy . . . It's a cuddly teddy, ah.' This is similar to the early conversation described above:

each time, I waited for the child to respond to what I was saying, either through their facial expression, their body language or a sound that they made.

Eventually these sounds turn into babbling (a repeating series of sounds that may sound like a baby is having a mini conversation). When my babies babbled, I tried to repeat back what I heard. This would encourage more babbling and would also encourage my babies to copy me.[4] It was great fun having this kind of copying game with my babies and it helped develop our bonding and my babies' interest in communication. Around this age, my babies started to use some gestures too, starting with waving bye bye, through reaching up to be picked up and even some attempts at some of the baby signs that I had introduced in our early conversations. (See later section on whether baby-signing is useful.)

When words did start to appear (around 12 months), they didn't sound like adult versions of words. As mentioned, the speech and language therapist's definition of a word is a set of sounds used consistently to mean the same thing. So, if my child said 'woo woo' instead of 'dog' in their early days, that was fine by me: I knew there were only a small number of people who really needed to understand what they were saying at this point. I would usually be around to translate, so I could say 'woof woof – yes it's a dog'. This meant that I was repeating the word that my child was using – reinforcing their attempt to communicate. I also gave them the adult version to copy when they were ready.

As my children used more words, there were often times when I didn't know what they were saying. All I could do was to look at what they appeared to be interested in, or what they had just experienced, and reflect back what I thought they might be talking about. For example, when a bus had just gone by and my child said 'wee ya', I thought that they might have been starting to sing the 'Wheels on the Bus' song, so I joined in too. I would say something like 'wee ya – yes, the wheels on the bus go round and round, round and round, round and round'. I thought that I had probably got it right if my child stopped saying their set of sounds and joined in with what I was doing (in this case, singing).

The more time that we spend with children and the more that we try to look at the world through their eyes, the better we are at interpreting what they are seeing and saying. When we reflect this back to them, they start to learn the adult versions of the words that they are trying to use.

Children are generally very forgiving if we don't get what they are saying immediately. They often don't seem to mind, as long as we have given it our best guess. If my children were very determined with their repetition of a set of sounds, and didn't join in with what I was doing next, I would generally realise that I hadn't understood them. If I still wasn't able to follow what they were saying, I had to be honest and say 'I'm not sure what you mean' and try and occupy them with something else.

As my children developed, I was able to shape the way that they formed words by responding with the adult version of the word for them to copy when they were ready. It is important that we don't ask children directly to repeat back what we are saying, as this doesn't actually help their ability to say words in an adult way (see above). They need to work it out for themselves.

Some children may have difficulties in the way that they use sounds: they may talk in the way that younger children talk and use some sounds in the wrong places. There are sections later in this guide focusing on speech sounds and also detailing how to support children with speech, language and communication needs.

What about dummies?

Dummies can be useful to help young children get to sleep. They are often recommended for young children who are colicky or difficult to soothe. Some research suggests that using a dummy when putting a baby down to sleep could reduce the risk of sudden infant death, although the evidence for this is limited. The Lullaby Trust[5] identifies some key pointers for dummy use:

- If you choose to use a dummy, wait until breastfeeding is well established (at up to about four weeks old).

- Stop giving a dummy to your baby to go to sleep between six and 12 months.

- Don't force your baby to take a dummy or put it back in if your baby spits it out.

- Don't use a neck cord.

- Don't put anything sweet on the dummy, and don't offer during awake time.

- Using an orthodontic dummy is best as it adapts to your baby's mouth shape.

- If you choose to use a dummy, make sure it is part of your baby's regular sleep routine.

Alongside these guidelines, it is thought that dummies can get in the way of both the development of words and the development of appropriate speech sounds if they are over-used.

There is a range of research which highlights negative impact of dummy-use on a child's language development. When we think about the meaning of the word 'dummy', it literally means 'to make silent'. Adults often use dummies when we want children to be quiet, perhaps because they are upset or grizzly. Sometimes, the dummy stays in the mouth when the child is happier. This can cause difficulties as children play with sounds less when they have a dummy in their mouth. This affects important sound-practice that the child needs for making words. It also means that the adult is less likely to respond to the sounds the child makes. This reduces the opportunity for the 'serve and return' interaction which we know is the basis for communication. The fewer sounds that the child makes, the fewer sounds that the adult makes and the child makes even fewer sounds in response.

Some people might be reading this and thinking 'That's great, I don't want my child to be making lots of noise.' The downside is if they don't practise the noises, the child will not be able to practise their words. Ultimately, this means that they are more likely to get frustrated and more likely to cry and scream when they can't make themselves understood.

Research shows that children who use dummies more frequently, and for longer periods of time, may have increased chances of ear infections. Ear infections are often very painful and can also cause hearing problems which can impact the development of talking (see section on hearing difficulties above).

Figure 4.1

Children who continue to use dummies in the day-time, especially when they are trying to talk around their dummies, often have speech sound difficulties, although there is recent research suggesting that these speech sound difficulties get better over time. Speech sounds such as 's', 't' and 'd' need the tongue tip to reach the part of the mouth just behind the front teeth. Other speech sounds such as 'p', 'b', 'm', f and 'v' require good movement of the lips. Both the lips and the front teeth are not so easy to move when there is a dummy in the way. As a speech and language therapist, I have seen many dummy-users who replace 'front' speech sounds (like 's', 't' and 'd') with 'back' speech sounds like 'k' and 'g'. This makes children's speech very hard to understand and can cause the child frustration and embarrassment if people aren't able to understand what they say. The sentence 'I wonk ga hag gume kokik' is much more difficult to understand than 'I want to have some chocolate'. You can test this out for yourself by holding a carrot in your mouth (as a child would hold a dummy) and try to have a conversation.

The recommendation for supporting good language development is that dummies should be kept to sleep-times only, although the UK British Dental Association advocates that dummy use should be stopped by one year old. It may be that older children who are very used to having a dummy get very cross when they are no longer allowed to have it. Being persistent as an adult in this situation (and ignoring the possible crying and temper tantrums) will ultimately pay off. The longer that you allow a child to have a dummy, the more difficult it will be to take away.

Handy hints

Children keeping hold of their dummies when they are over one year old can be difficult to stop. NHS Scotland suggest ideas that other parents have tried, including:

– Give the dummy/bottle to Santa or the tooth fairy.
– Swap the dummy/bottle for a gift/cuddly toy/new toothbrush.
– Agree with your child to throw the dummy/bottle in the bin.[1]

Do children benefit from screen time?

Many people use screen time as a way of entertaining a child, when there is something else the adult has to do, or to manage a difficult or tiring situation. If this does happen, it is important to be aware of limiting screen time as much as possible.

The World Health Organization published guidelines in 2019[6] identifying that children under two years should not be exposed to any screen time at all. They also recommend that older children, between two and five, should be limited to no more than an hour of screen time each day. There are a number of reasons for this, including that children are, by nature, active, and sitting still, often for a long time, in front of a TV, tablet or phone increases the likelihood of childhood obesity.

When thinking about using screens to entertain young children, there are some questions that can be asked. For example, who is benefitting most from the child using the screen – the adult or the child? Young children (under three and a half to four) have short attention spans (often less than five–ten minutes). They are unable to follow long, complicated storylines and often don't understand long and complex sentences. Despite this, there may be encouragement for toddlers to watch feature-length films, or even cartoons of 15 minutes or so. It may well be that rather than understanding the story, the child is mesmerised by flashing lights and different voices.

Research has identified that screen time can impact on a child's development, [7] quality of sleep[8] and brain development. One of the biggest downsides of screens, in terms of language development, is that they don't respond to a child's interests, gaze and attempts to communicate the way that an adult does: time on screen is time away from talking with a responsive adult who has much better skills to support communication development.

Alternatives to screen time include giving a child a book to look at or putting a young child in their high-chair or baby bouncer and talking to them about the household tasks that you are doing. Sometimes, the household tasks can wait and you could go out for a walk together instead.

What toys do they need?

Of all the items that I have used as a speech and language therapist, a bottle of bubble mixture has been the most useful. I have even entertained a child on a train that was stuck outside a station with a bottle of bubbles I had in my bag! I'm not sure if the child was more interested in the bubbles, or the fact that someone was playing with them when their parents were getting anxious about their delayed journey.

Children don't need expensive toys as much as they need someone to play with. In fact, the best toy a child can have is a responsive adult. Think how much fun a child has when playing 'peep-bo', being tickled, told a made-up story, or being rocked or gently swung.

When playing with children, adults can use any safe household object. This can include pans for banging, cardboard boxes to become a pretend boat, paper envelopes to make hats or puppets, the world around us to investigate.

And children who learn to pretend that one thing is another (a set of chairs together to make a bus, or a blanket over a table to make a den) will learn the power of imagination. This kind of creativity provides plenty of opportunity for having fun together and also helps with later development at school.

Children can enjoy playing with any silly old thing . . . just have fun together with the child.

Household objects that I have used with my children and those I have worked with include:

- shoe boxes for posting things into or hiding things in;
- plastic bottles filled with different items to make shakers;
- kitchen rolls or cardboard tubes to make into trumpets;
- envelopes to make into puppets;
- rolled up paper for a ball;
- a broom to pretend to fly with;
- keys to jingle;
- alarm clocks to hide and search for when the alarm goes off;
- shells, conkers and even bottle tops to collect as 'treasure'.

The list is endless. The key is making sure that each item is safe for the age of the child and to show the child that these objects are fun to play with.

The job of toy manufacturers and sellers is to persuade us that their toy is the best for helping children's learning and that no Christmas or birthday is complete without their particular item. Their business depends on us believing them, but really it's not true.

Is baby-signing helpful?

When most adults talk, they gesture. These gestures can become very animated, particularly when there are strong emotions involved. Gestures help to emphasise what we are saying, as they can be seen alongside the words that are heard.

This is the basis for baby-signing. It is based on the natural gestures that we all use and that babies start to use before they talk. The aim of baby-signing is to support the development of talking, not to replace it.

As a speech and language therapist, when working with children who struggle to understand and use words clearly, I use a signing system called Makaton. Makaton is used, alongside the spoken words, to emphasise key words in speech in the order that the words are spoken. It is different to British Sign Language (used by deaf communicators), as BSL is a language in its own right, with different word order to English.

The organisation that has developed Makaton identifies that 'Research has shown that signs and gestures are easier to learn than spoken words. This makes sense: Babies use gestures before they can speak, to tell us what they want. For example, they might point at the biscuit tin or hold out their arms to be lifted up.' [9]

If adults use baby-signing or Makaton to support language development, it must be used alongside spoken words too.

Because I used Makaton as a speech and language therapist, with other people's children, it came very naturally for me to use it with my own children when they were learning to talk. Some advantages of this, or other forms of baby-signing, are:

- It helps reduce the length of the sentences we use with children, as our knowledge of signs is much less than our knowledge of spoken words

- It helps to ensure that we are face to face with children when we communicate with them

- The sign can be attempted by the child often before they are able to attempt to say the equivalent word

- A single sign might replace a range of spoken words, e.g. 'cup', 'drink', 'glass', 'beaker' all have the same sign

- A sign, made at the same time as the word is spoken, provides two forms of information for a child to focus on, using two senses – hearing and seeing.

Many, many children learn to communicate without the support of signing. It is important not to feel that 'this is something else that I have to do'. You can use your usual gestures or respond to a child's gestures by interpreting them and saying the word that seems to fit. This is a useful way of supporting them to learn to talk.

If you do want to find out about baby-signing, there are lots of useful organisations (Signalong, Sing and Sign etc.), books, websites and classes that you can find locally.

Can music and singing help too?

Recent research confirms the long-held belief that music is good for children's development. Music helps develop listening skills. It leads to strong emotional reactions that can be harnessed to support learning and it is also used to support bonding and interaction. Additionally, we know that many features of music and singing support language development.

Many parents, early years practitioners, childminders and speech and language therapists use songs, rhymes and music to support children to learn to talk. Songs are repetitive, interesting to children, often have actions and they promote fundamental listening skills.

They are also great for sharing attention with children – even if only one of you is actually singing at one time.

Singing helps language development for children in a range of ages: young children can be encouraged to carry out the songs' actions (think of 'Row, row, row the boat'). They can also join in with the last word in a song (e.g. 'Twinkle twinkle little star, how I wonder what you......'. Older children can also find new rhyming words for a missing line in a song. For example, 'When I was three, I climbed a tree. When I was four, I ... (encourage the child to think of a rhyme)'.

Toddlers and very young children are particularly interested in the repetitive nature of many pre-school songs. This helps them in learning to use language to predict what comes next, also in developing vocabulary. It can be especially helpful for children learning English as an additional language.

By the time children get to pre-school and school, they can be encouraged to listen to rhythm and rhyme. They will start to copy sound sequences and think about which words rhyme. These skills help children's ability to produce speech sounds and to break words up into their constituent parts – a vital skill for reading.

You can use any type of music to sing to – traditional rhymes, pop songs or rap. Whether it's singing together, beating out rhythms with a saucepan lid and a wooden spoon or learning to play the drums, it's all important in eventually learning to communicate well through words.

Key points from this chapter

Tuning into a child, watching what they are interested in and commenting on what they are doing is useful in understanding them. This helps you to interpret their gurgles and start early conversations.

Playing together, signing and singing are all valuable ways of helping children's language to develop.

Hearing difficulties, screen time and dummies can get in the way of good language development opportunities.

Notes

1 www.nhs.uk/conditions/glue-ear/
2 https://www.entuk.org/grommets
3 'Talking baby at 3 months old', https://www.youtube.com/watch?v=vm37vKnDdh8
4 '9 month old baby talking: Just say "Mama"', https://tinyurl.com/yjatktef

5 www.lullabytrust.org.uk

6 World Health Organization (2019) Guidelines on Physical Activity, Sedentary Behaviour and Sleep for Children under 5 Years of Age

7 Madigan, S, Browne, D, Racine, N, Mori, C and Tough, S (2019) Association between screen time and children's performance on a developmental screening test. *JAMA Pediatr.* (Mar 1)173(3): 244–250. doi:10.1001/jamapediatrics.2018.5056

8 Cheung, C H, Bedford, R, Saez De Urabain, I R, Karmiloff-Smith, A and Smith, T J (2017) Daily touchscreen use in infants and toddlers is associated with reduced sleep and delayed sleep onset. *Scientific Reports*, 7:46104. https://www.ncbi.nlm.nih.gov/pmc/articles/PMC5390665/

9 www.makaton.org

Chapter five

WHAT IF THINGS AREN'T GOING TO PLAN?

In this chapter, we will cover

- A note on the stresses and strains of parenthood and childcare

- Concerns about speech, language and communication development not going as expected

- Where to get support for speech, language and communication development

- The role of speech and language therapists.

Parenting and childcare is hard work

Whilst this book is about supporting adults to help children to find their voices, working with children and, in particular, parenthood can take up a lot of your thinking space.

Some parents (although they are few and far between) will bond straight away with their babies and have supportive families and children who sleep all night. They may have secure financial positions and take to parenthood straightaway. For the rest of us, this is a dream which is very far from reality. Tiredness and making space for another little person in our lives causes its own stresses and strains. This, combined with possible post-natal depression, financial worries, competing demands of other adults and children and, for some, domestic violence, substance use and other medical or mental health conditions, means that many, many parents struggle with getting through each day.

If you are one of the parents with some difficulties, described above, you are not alone. Do seek help from friends and family, if you can. Also take advantage of the professional groups who are around to help you – health visitors, children's centres, family hubs, GPs. They are all there to support you in the task that you are taking on. With help, you will achieve. You will make it through and you will learn so much along the way. You will learn about your child,

DOI: 10.4324/9781003242840-6

Figure 5.1

about yourself, about how you make a difference to your child's learning. You will learn about the positive impact that you can have on another person's life, even when your own is tough to handle sometimes.

Remember, none of us is a perfect person and none of us is a perfect parent – what I hope is that you will learn from this book. I hope that you will put into practice what you can, with the aim of helping to make your child a successful communicator.

My experience is that the time you put in reaps rewards for both parents and children.

I think there might be a problem

Some children struggle with learning to communicate, even though they have someone around them doing all the right things.

Children might have difficulties in:

- understanding words and sentences,
- finding the right words to express themselves,

- making adult speech sounds,

- and / or knowing what to say when.

Approximately 10% of all children will have ongoing difficulties in one or more of these areas above. In these cases, early identification and support is really important.

In 2008, a review of support for children with speech, language and communication needs (SLCN)[1] identified a lack of information for parents and early years practitioners about children's communication development. Since this time, a range of organisations have produced lots of information available about how children develop communication skills and at what ages. The children's communication charity, I CAN, provides 'Ages and Stages of Speech, Language and Communication Development' posters for professionals, as well as 'First Words' posters for parents. The charity's 'Universally Speaking' is a great guide to communication development for early years practitioners. There is also an on-line progress checker available on https://ican.org.uk/i-cans-talking-point/progress-checker-home. (Additional links are provided at the end of this guide).

If there are concerns about a child's communication and language development, talk to someone. As a parent, you could talk to another member of your family, a trusted friend, an early years practitioner or a health visitor. As an early years practitioner or childminder, talk over your concerns with colleagues and with the child's parents. It is important not to let someone reassure you if you are convinced that there is a delay. If you are concerned, you will often be right – children's speech and language skills are best supported as early as possible. Using the progress checker highlighted above can help too.

If a child does have a delay in their speech, language and communication development, it is important to have their skills assessed by a professional. Some early years settings use screening tools such as WellComm or Teddy Talk Test and some support children with delayed language development through interventions such as Early Talk Boost or the Nuffield Early Language Intervention.

Finding out more about the child's development

As a parent or a practitioner working with children, you will be watching to see how the child develops. If you are worried about their communication skills, keep a note of what the child is doing – what they understand, how they get their message across.

Watch for how a child responds to sentences and questions that are out of context, or unfamiliar. For example, will a child find their shoes when it is time to go to bed, or a toy in another room?

Listen to the number of words that a child typically puts together in a sentence. How does this compare to the milestones guide in Chapter One?

Areas to consider are:

- **The child's understanding of language:** Does he /she follow instructions on his or her own, as well as in a group? What happens if these instructions are out of the normal routine, e.g. at snack time? You could say 'Go and get your coat' and see what happens. You could also try asking about pictures in a book. The type of question that you ask will depend on the child's age e.g. 'Can you see the duck?' (for a one or two-year-old), 'Which one is kicking the ball?' (for a two or three-year-old) or 'Can you find the small blue bucket?' (for a three- or four-year-old).

- **Use of words and sentences:** What length of sentences does the child use? Is what the child is talking about relevant to what is going on around them? Does the child use the right level of grammar and linking words such as 'but' and 'if' (three- and four-year-olds)?

- **Speech sounds**: Does the child use a range of speech sounds? Is their speech easy to understand? If not, can you work out which sounds are used and which are not? How does this relate to what the child is expected to do for their age? (see earlier milestone guide and useful links at the end of this guide).

Stuttering / stammering / dysfluency

About 5% of toddlers repeat sounds, syllables or words when they talk. Two of my three children did the same at around three or four years old.

This 'dysfluency' in toddler talk may last for a few days or months, or occur sporadically. It may stay for a while, then disappear, then come back again. This is perfectly normal and usually happens when a child has a lot that they want to say but doesn't yet have a large enough vocabulary to really express themselves. [2]

If a child is showing concern about the way that they talk, or if a parent is very concerned, contact your local speech and language therapy department. The British Stammering Association has useful tips on their website for ways in which the adult can adapt their talk. This will help to take pressure off a child who is going through the normal stage of dysfluency.[3] It is important not to draw the child's attention to how they are talking or ask them to slow down or stop to think about what they are going to say. Instead:

1 **Show the child that you are interested in what they say, not how they say it.** Try to maintain natural eye-contact. Don't finish the child's sentences – this can be frustrating for the child.

2 **Be supportive.** Respond to the dysfluency in the same way that you would with any other difficulties that arise, such as when they trip over or spill things. If you feel it's appropriate, acknowledge the difficulty in a matter-of-fact way. Avoid labelling the difficulty as 'stammering' or 'stuttering'. Instead, use expressions like 'bumpy speech' or 'getting stuck', or let the child describe what's happening in their own words.

3 **If you speak quickly, slow down your own rate of speech when you talk to the child.** Pausing for a second before you answer or ask the child a question can also help them to feel less rushed.

4 **Be encouraging if the child gets upset about their talking, just as you would if they were upset about any other difficulty.** Say something like 'Don't worry, talking can be tricky sometimes when you're still learning.'

5 **Observe the child's speaking patterns but try to resist seeing them as a 'problem'.** Stammering is not caused by adults, but your anxiety can be passed on to the child. They may begin to feel they are doing something 'wrong'. In fact, this stage may well pass.

6 **Set aside a few minutes at a regular time each day when you can give your full attention to the child in a calm, relaxed atmosphere.** Follow their lead in playing or talking about something they like. The top tips in Chapter Two will help in this.

7 **Reduce the number of questions you ask.** This way, the child is less likely to feel under pressure. Keep your sentences short and simple and instead of asking questions, simply comment on what the child has said, letting them know that you're listening.

8 **Encourage everyone to take turns to talk so that everyone can talk without being interrupted.** This will reduce the pressure that each person might feel when speaking.

9 **Respond to the child's behaviour as you would with a child who is talking easily.**

10 **Try to avoid a hectic and rushed timetable.** Dysfluency can increase when children are tired. All children respond well to a routine and structured environment, with regular sleep patterns and a regular, healthy diet.

Getting the right support

There are lots of people around who might help you to get the right support for a child's communication development. It is important that you trust your gut instinct and that, if you are concerned about a child, you keep going until you get the help you need.

Health visitors are being trained to support parents to enable their children to develop good language skills. Many early years practitioners and childminders can also give parents support in this area. Children's centres and family hubs often run speech and language groups that can be accessed by a range of children and families.

Figure 5.2

In some early years settings, particular early interventions (such as those mentioned above) are available. It is important that the interventions that are used are tried and tested and that we are certain that they make a difference to children's speech and language development.

Some children may need more significant input, particularly if they have a severe or complex speech, language and communication need, or another special educational need or disability affecting their communication and interaction. In this case, referral to your local speech and language therapy department would be helpful.

Speech and language therapists

Speech and language therapists are professionals who work with children and adults to support all aspects of communication and swallowing difficulties. Many children's difficulties can be resolved with support from early years settings. Others may need a short burst of speech and language therapy support over a few months. Some children will need support that goes on for a few years and some children may have a lifelong difficulty.

Identifying what type of difficulty a child may have and getting support as early as possible is very important.

A referral to a speech and language therapist can be made by anyone with parents' permission – in most areas. You don't have to go through a health visitor or GP if there are concerns. NHS Speech and Language Therapy departments do have criteria for referral. You can usually find out if a child meets this, by looking on-line for your area or contacting the local speech and language therapy department. Waiting lists for assessment can be long (at least three months) so it is important to follow up concerns as soon as they are identified.

Once the child's communication skills have been assessed by a speech and language therapist, they will let you know whether the child has a difficulty and how you can work together to support the child.

Some early years settings or parents may have access to independent speech and language therapists who will charge for their services. To find out about an independent speech and language therapist near you, go to www.helpwithtalking.com.

Key points from this chapter

A child not reaching their milestones may have speech, language and communication needs. They may be able to access support through programmes run in early years settings, children's centres or family hubs. Or they may need to see a speech and language therapist.

If there are concerns about how a child is developing their talking, it is important to seek help.

Notes

1 The Bercow Report: A review of services for children and young people (0–19) with speech, language and communication needs. Digital Education Resource Archive (DERA) (ioe.ac.uk), https://dera.ioe.ac.uk/8405/7/7771-dcsf-bercow_Redacted.pdf
2 www.whattoexpect.com/toddler-development/toddler-speech.aspx
3 https://stamma.org/get-support/parents

Chapter six

NEXT STEPS

In this chapter you will learn about

- later language development

- speech sounds

- getting ready for nursery or school

- more information for parents

- more information for early years practitioners, including childminders.

Two words and beyond

Joining words together is a very, very important step in a child's early language development. This step takes a child from being able to name individual objects or actions to being able to describe what's going on, what has gone on and what might happen next. Linking more than one word together provides the framework for linking more than one idea together and from there, as they say 'the world is your oyster'. This communication skill is the beginning of the child being able to develop language for thinking, learning, building relationships and reading and writing.

Many children, once they have understood how words can link together, really make significant progress with their ability to understand and talk. The 'vocabulary explosion' is a significant event. This is found to happen typically between 18 months and two years. At this time, many toddlers are learning ten or more words a day, helping them move towards the adult vocabulary of approximately 50,000 words!

Every time a child hears a new word, they start to learn a little bit more about it. And every time they learn a word, they have a new mechanism for hooking on new words to the existing

DOI: 10.4324/9781003242840-7

concept.[1] This is known as 'fast mapping' and is the same skill that is used to learn a foreign language, once one language is known. You may have noticed that people who speak more than one language seem to find it easier to learn three, four or even five. This is the reason why – being good at understanding and using words helps us to be even better at understanding and using more words.

Communication skills can grow at such a fast rate that, by the time a typically developing child gets to school, they have the skills to:

- Understand spoken instructions without stopping what they are doing to look at the speaker

- Take turns in much longer conversations

- Understand more complicated language such as 'first', 'last', 'might', 'maybe', 'above' and 'in between'

- Understand words that describe sequences such as 'first we are going to the shop, next we will play in the park'

- Use sentences that are well formed. However, they may still have some difficulties with grammar. For example, saying 'sheeps' instead of 'sheep' or 'goed' instead of 'went'

- Think more about the meanings of words, such as describing the meaning of simple words or asking what a new word means.[2]

Handy hints

Children learn new words when they are said in simple sentences in context. Help children to understand and use longer sentences, with new vocabulary, by using sentences that are generally one word longer than the child uses.

Children who hear a particular word repeated a number of times, in a range of different contexts, will find it easier to understand what this word means. They will then use it themselves when they are ready.

With children in the pre-school year or in the early years of school, think about which new everyday words you could teach a child each week.

Speech sound development

When children are first learning to talk, they simplify the words that they are using because using adult speech sounds is just too complicated at this early stage. They start with sounds that are easy to say such as 'm', 'b', 'd', 't', 'p', 'w' and all the vowels ('a', 'e', 'i' 'o', 'u', 'oo', 'ah', 'ee', 'ay' etc.).

By the time a child is around three years old, their range of speech sounds increases to include sounds such as 'f', 'dge', 's', 'z' etc., although very frequently at this age, children have not learned to tell the difference between key sounds and so they are not using them correctly in their own conversations.[3]

Most four-year-olds can be relatively easily understood by people outside of their direct family, having learnt to tell the difference between different sounds and to use them in their own speech.

Speech sound development is the 'icing on the cake'. A child who is not yet using words and sentences at the level expected for their age will also not be using speech sounds appropriately. However, it is important to get the range of words and sentences right before we worry about speech sounds at this point.

When children have developed a good level of understanding and are using words and sentences, then we can focus on getting their speech sounds right.

To help a child to develop their speech sounds, avoid correcting what they are saying, or asking them to repeat words, sounds or chunks of words after you. Instead, repeat back to the child, in a positive way, the word they are trying to say, e.g. Child: 'I can see a dut.' Adult: 'Oh, you can see a duck. What a lovely duck. Quack quack quack.' This provides an opportunity for the child to hear the word that they are attempting and will help them to get it right another time, when they are ready.

Listening activities such as described in the Letters and Sounds programme at phase 1 will also help.[4]

Some children who have a good level of words and sentences will still struggle with their speech sound development. If trying the tips above don't work, they may need the specialist support of a speech and language therapist.

Getting ready for nursery and school

Nowadays, many children will have started nursery, or another form of childcare, in the first or second year of their life. This means that many children have a good understanding about what it's like spending time with someone who is not a member of their household. However, having a child about to start nursery can be a worrying time for parents (although often not for the child). This can be more about adults' anxieties than children's. Think about what might be a cause for concern and how you can best reassure yourself.

Visiting a childcare or education setting is important. Most settings include one or more 'getting to know you' sessions, where the child can spend short amounts of time in the new environment. This also helps the staff in the setting to get to know the child, as well as giving the parent an opportunity to practice being an adult without a child attached (this can feel very strange the first time!).

Most childcare and education settings have a particular routine that they try to stick to each day. This helps the child to know what to expect and also helps the adults to structure their days. Preparation and planning will help a child to settle in. This will also help the adults who are working with a particular child to get to know their needs.

As a parent looking at childcare or education environments, it is important to consider how the setting will communicate with you about your child; what they are good at and what areas they might need to focus on. Look out for adults who are able to build a strong bond with the children in their care and who want to work with you as parents to provide the best for the child.

As an early years practitioner or teacher, think about how you can find out what the child is like at home, how you can get to know the parent and how you share information about the child. Some settings use a 'communication passport'[5] to find out about the child, or to pass information about the child's communication skills to the next group, or to school.

There are many sources of information about getting ready for school and nursery, e.g.

- Getting Ready for School/Nursery Information Sheet (nhsggc.org.uk)[6]
- School Readiness Checklist (buckshealthcare.nhs.uk)[7]
- Parents Guide to School Readiness (Childcare.co.uk)[8]

It is worth looking at these in plenty of time to help prepare the child (and the adult) for moving on to the next stage. Your local authority may well have a school readiness checklist that you as a parent, or early years practitioner can work towards.

Anything else I should know (parents)

In my experience, other parents are a great source of support. I know that there are many aspects of being a parent that I would not have managed without the support of my friends who also had children of around the same age.

However, it can be difficult to know who to believe and what other parents are basing their advice on. Is it technical knowledge, parental experience or wishes and hopes and something that they may have heard (inaccurately) from someone else?

Unfortunately, I have also had some (relatively rare) experience of professionals who have less than adequate knowledge and have given inaccurate advice to families that I have been working with. As I say, this is rare, but it is often worth 'triangulating' information that you hear. Is the information coming from more than one source and does it link with information that is provided by organisations with specialist knowledge and experience?

There is now lots of information available on the internet from reputable organisations who have specific knowledge in helping children to learn to talk – a list of these is available at the end of this guide. Use this guide and the links to other organisations well and ensure that you are equipped, in advance, to deal with the range of experiences that you have with your child – remember they weren't born with an instruction manual!

Anything else I should know (all early years practitioners)

As you are aware, the current Early Years Foundation Stage in England has a significant focus on communication and language, as one of the prime areas on which all other skills are based. Your professional qualifications and experience may already have provided you with lots of useful knowledge. There is also plenty of specific training around, much of which is funded by the Department for Education, although this will change over time.

Make sure that you get your information from people who know: Public Health England have produced some useful information for health visitors that can also be accessed by early years practitioners. Other organisations are listed at the end of the guide.

Key areas to consider in supporting children's communication and language are:

- Do you know what to expect at what ages for typically developing children?
- How do you adjust your own language to support the language development of the children that you work with?
- How can you build language development activities into your daily routines?
- How do you identify children with speech, language and communication needs (SLCN)?
- What interventions can you provide within your setting to support children with SLCN?

- How do you work with parents to share messages with them about communication and language development, and any additional needs that individual children have?

- How do you link with local speech and language therapy services?

- Have you carried out an audit of your setting – what works well and less well to support children's communication and language development in your setting?[9]

Don't just take it from me – what do other people say?

In my research for this guide, I was lucky enough to have access to a group of parents, all with children who were babies, toddlers and pre-schoolers. The following words are direct quotes from these parents, although their names have been changed:

Geena: *'You absolutely need to just keep communicating with your babies even when they are too young to speak. Have them around you and family and friends so they hear various conversations their whole life, even . . . songs all help them hear and learn new words and sentences. You need to know every child is different so they may have set guidelines and milestones of what a child should be doing at each age, but ultimately they do it at their own pace. You shouldn't compare them too heavily to other people's children the same age, but also if you do have your own concerns about your child's talking you should know it isn't shameful to speak to your health worker or doctor or your child's school, as they will have definitely dealt with similar things before and know the right route to go to help your kids talk if they are having trouble.'*

Raj: *'Given Joseph is – and always had been – a late bloomer in the speech department, I wish I had clearer guidance on what was 'expected' and what counted as 'delayed' – one website can say expect 10 words at x age, the next says they're behind if they aren't speaking 50 by that time. Of course they all do things at different times but there was conflicting advice on when to actually be concerned. That would have been helpful! Also a toddler-to-adult translator, like common words they mispronounce. It's tough when I can't make out what he means. He keeps saying 'day sem ba' at the moment, but I don't think he's saying December!'*

Tania: *'They're listening all the time and absorb like sponges – don't use words you don't want them to when they can hear! They love repetition, so get ready to sing the same song or read the same story or say the same silly phrase 50 times.'*

Bud: *'I think for me rather than 'teaching' let them take the lead if they love a certain song or program use that to your advantage and try [to] get them to say words or learn the little songs. Also the actions that went with songs is good that I learnt with Adalind . . . she started with the hand actions then I figured out what [she was] trying to tell me so [I] started saying the word or words that went with and she's bloomed from there.'*

Figure 6.1

Key points from this chapter

There is a lot that you can do to help build a child's communication skills for school. Typically developing five-year-olds have quite complex language skills, with speech sounds that are still developing.

Remember to use the links and resources that you have as a parent, childminder or early years practitioner, including your friends and colleagues.

Talk to other people about their experiences of children's communication. And find out as much as you can from a range of published resources.

Notes

1 McMurray, B (2007) Defusing the Childhood Vocabulary Explosion. *Science* (Aug 3) 317(5838): 613 doi:10.1126/science.1144073
2 Ages and Stages (ican.org.uk), https://ican.org.uk/i-cans-talking-point/parents/ages-and-stages/
3 https://www.oxfordhealth.nhs.uk/wp-content/uploads/docs/speech-sound-development-chart.pdf

4 Letters and Sounds: Principles and practice of high quality phonics. Phase One Teaching, https:// assets.publishing.service.gov.uk/government/uploads/system/uploads/attachment_data/ file/190537/Letters_and_Sounds_-_Phase_One.pdfProgramme (publishing.service.gov.uk)

5 Transition resource. I CAN.FINAL.pdf (councilfordisabledchildren.org.uk), https:// councilfordisabledchildren.org.uk/sites/default/files/uploads/Transition%20resource.I%20CAN. FINAL.pdf

6 www.nhsggc.org.uk/media/257792/getting-ready-for-school-or-nursery-information-sheet.pdf

7 https://www.buckshealthcare.nhs.uk/cyp/wp-content/uploads/sites/6/2021/05/school-readiness- checklist-1.pdf

8 www.childcare.co.uk/information/school-readiness

9 SLCN Quick Review Checklist, https://councilfordisabledchildren.org.uk/what-we-do-0/networks/ early-years-send/early-years-send-partnership-resources/speech-language-and-3

FURTHER INFORMATION

Useful websites

Afasic – Charity supporting families and children with speech, language and communication needs: https://www.afasic.org.uk

BBC's campaign to support early communication skills: https://www.bbc.co.uk/tiny-happy-people

BBC parenting website: http://www.bbc.co.uk/parenting/

Chat, play read national campaign: https://theinstituteofwellbeing.com/chatplayread

I CAN, the Children's Communication Charity: https://www.ican.org.uk

Information about children's development and how to help: https://hungrylittleminds.campaign.gov.uk

Lucid – The ESRC International Centre for Language and Communication Development: http://www.lucid.ac.uk/

National Literacy Trust: https://literacytrust.org.uk

National Literacy Trust's family reading information: http://literacytrust.org.uk/familyreading/parents/index.html

Talking Point – Information on everything to do with speech, language and communication: https://www.ican.org.uk/i-cans-talking-point

The Communication Trust – Organisation supporting teachers and practitioners working with children's communication development and needs: https://ican.org.uk/i-cans-talking-point/professionals/tct-resources/

Video resource – Short films showing how a child might want an adult to communicate with them: Through the Eyes of a Child, https://ican.org.uk/i-cans-talking-point/professionals/tct-resources/through-the-eyes-of-a-child/

Words for Life Activities for learning and language development from birth to 12 years: https://wordsforlife.org.uk/

DOI: 10.4324/9781003242840-8

Information in books for parents and practitioners

Johnson's Everyday Babycare (2004) *Learning to Talk*. Gardners Books

Jones, M (2015) *Talking and Learning with Young Children*. Sage Publications

Hirsch-Pacek, K and Michnick Golinkoff, R (2004) *Einstein Never Used Flash Cards: How our children really learn – and why they need to play more and memorize less*. Rodale

Gross, J (2018) *Time to Talk: Implementing outstanding practice in speech, language and communication*. Routledge

Murray, L and Andrews, L (2005) *The Social Baby: Understanding babies' communication from birth*. The Children's Project

Ward, S (2001) *Baby Talk: Strengthen your child's ability to listen, understand, and communicate*. Ballantine Books

Acknowledgements

Photography, in order of appearance

Gabe Pierce

Tina Floersch

Kelly Sikkema

Kate Freeman

Yogendra Singh

Muhammad Murtaza Ghani

Picsea

Sandy Innocent

Iiona Virgin

Zachary Kadolph

Colin May

Sandy Innocent

Kate Freeman

Rendy Novantino

My grateful thanks also go to . . .

. . . Jenny Edge, without whom, the 'Words Together' series would still be a set of words and toys without illustration.

Also, to those who listened to me, inspired and supported me and gave me insights and advice for this guide, especially Pete Flliott, Jaquie Eames, Hazel Blenkinsop, Susie Gowers, Shiela Freeman, Clive Freeman, Harvey Innocent, Sandy Innocent, Chay Innocent, Tina Lamb, the Acutt family, Jack Elliott and Talia Wood.

Additional books in the 'Words Together' series

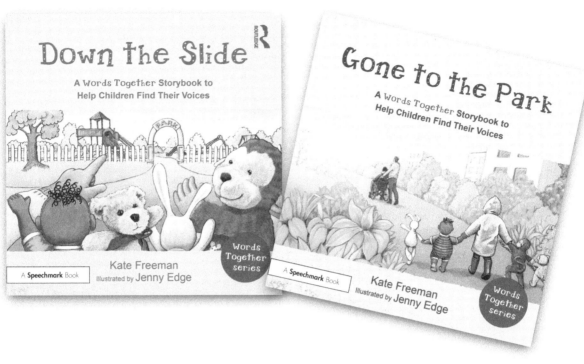

INDEX